D0007368

THE LOST ART
OF CROSS-EXAMINATION

or

Perjury Anyone?

The Lost Art
of Cross-Examination

or Perjury Anyone?

by J. W. EHRLICH

WITH A FOREWORD BY *Percy Foreman*

BARNES
&NOBLE
BOOKS
NEW YORK

This edition published by Barnes & Noble, Inc.,
by arrangement with the Putnam Publishing Group Inc.

1993 Barnes & Noble Books

ISBN 0-88029-151-6

Printed and bound in the United States of America

M 9 8 7 6 5

Contents

Contents

Foreword

WHEN a key witness for the prosecution is cornered into hedging or saying, "I don't know," the defending trial lawyer has achieved the first, essential act of the defense —to cast a shadow of doubt over the validity of the prosecution's testimony.

The strategy of cross-examination is not and probably never will be a science. It remains an art for the simplest of reasons: the most sophisticated computer we can envisage couldn't possibly cope with the unpredictable behavior of the witness under oath. Nor would the computer be any more effective in the role of the examiner who must catch both the overt blunders and the delicately camouflaged discrepancies in his adversary's testimony. And, more than simply recognize them, he must make capital of them with all the drama inherent in a precisely timed wave of the hand or an archly taunting tone of voice. "Then, sir, you really don't know, do you?"

If he is to win his case, the lawyer must catch these

7

slips and turn them back on the witness as weapons. Invariably, the defense lawyer's finest opportunities to demolish the effectiveness of the key witness in the minds of the court and jury come from the mouth of the witness himself—if the lawyer has the wits to recognize them and the skill to use them.

In short, the defending lawyer's first step in establishing that vital "reasonable doubt" regarding the guilt of his client is to establish reasonable doubt of the validity of the testimony presented by the opposition's key witness.

This is as it should be, for neither the life nor the freedom nor the fortunes of any man should hang on testimony of doubtful accuracy.

This is no book for the dilettante. But the judge, the lawyer, and the genuinely interested layman will find it stimulating, instructive, and even entertaining—each to his own taste.

It is an inspiring, yet eminently practical demonstration of the strategy and tactics of cross-examination which mark the difference between winning and losing in court. And let no one forget that, if the verdict goes against him, it matters not how diligently the lawyer has prepared his defense or with what zeal he pursues his adversary. His conscientious labor, his dramatic appeals to the hearts of the jurymen—and his worth to his client—add up to zero.

Jake Ehrlich is a man who relishes a fight. No one who has seen him in action can doubt it. But there's another and less well-known facet of this man which might help explain the genesis of his gentlemanly, yet devastating courtroom performances.

Aside from his devotion to family and friend, this man's early loves were the law and, of all things, boxing —and not as a spectator. By day, he devoured treatises on law and science and the humanities. On fight nights, he climbed into the professional ring and toughened his knuckles and sharpened his wits for pay. And those of us who know his story still recall the amazing spectacle of the young man who passed his bar examinations, embarked on the lofty calling of the law—and went on for two more years, clouting and being clouted in the ring.

With scholarly devotion, he has examined man's continuing effort to regulate his society for the common good. From the dictates of Moses to the teachings of Montesquieu, who laid the pattern of law as wc of the West practice it today, to the refinements and near absurdities of the twentieth century, this man has displayed an unquenchable thirst to know. This accounts for the fact that he so frequently obliterates those degreed and anointed pundits who have too easily gained recognition as authorities on life or literature or the laws devised by God and man.

Of the myriad cases tried and won by Jake Ehrlich, two come readily to mind as prime examples of the art of defeating the prosecution by annihilating the key witness. They are worthy of study for their sameness—and their dissimilarity. Sameness in strategy, dissimilarity in tactics.

In each instance, destruction of faith in the prosecution's testimony was achieved by the introduction of material artfully designed to take the opposition by surprise. And behind these courtroom maneuverings was a plentiful labor of research into the prosecution's probable approach.

In the Billie Holiday case, Ehrlich swung the jury in a matter of seconds with a piece of inadmissible evidence. In the *Howl* case, he did it by slowly and systematically destroying the counterfeit image of the prosecution's key witness as an authority on literature.

The Lost Art of Cross-Examination is a culmination of nearly a half century of study and practice by one of the great trial lawyers of this century.

It is a practical and inspiring revelation of the underlying principles of cross-examination. Imaginatively conceived and continually interesting, it is different from anything written about this art.

This book includes many shrewd insights, brilliant formulations, and challenging interpretations which will no doubt be discussed and debated by judges, intelligent laymen, and lawyers. It is a new study which is entertaining and stimulating.

PERCY FOREMAN

And the judges shall make diligent inquisition: and, behold, if the witness be a false witness, and hath testified falsely against his brother; then shall ye do unto him, as he had thought to have done unto his brother. . . .

Deuteronomy 19:18–19

THE LOST ART
OF CROSS-EXAMINATION

or

Perjury Anyone?

Truth

THE man who speaks truthfully may in fact say what is false, just as the man whose intent is to falsify may inadvertently speak the truth. Lying consists in saying the contrary of what one thinks or believes, and the withholding of truth is sometimes a worse deception than a direct lie.

The justice which courts administer is dependent on human facts. When the facts fail in accuracy, justice fails.

Many people think that we can create and operate legal tribunals which will have none of the weaknesses of the creators or operators. Because of this, it is necessary that evidence presented in court be as accurate as possible.

Men are prevented from discovering the exact truth by five basic causes: ignorance; arrogance; the difficulty of the subject; want of capacity to comprehend; and habit and training.

It is known that the form of a question has some effect on the truth of the reply. If one form of question is used, the answer may tend to be more truthful than if another form is used. By various details of its construction the question may convey implications, suggest replies, or eliminate alternatives.

It is sad, yet true that some people have little or no regard for their oaths and will commit perjury.

There is also the perjury of the witness who feels that some wrong has been done and will testify for the injured party. He will enlist his feelings in what he believes to be a righteous cause, and this automatically prompts him to color his testimony.

Few people possess the ability to be good liars. It is difficult to hide the outward manifestation of inner guilt. The amateur liar, who lacks the technique of the professional, may be usually recognized as such by an inability to meet the eyes of the examining lawyer, by squinting, by twitching the muscles of the face, by blushing, by constant swallowing, by cold sweat, by an extreme or unusual nervousness, by volubility, by overexplanation, or by a peculiar tone of voice.

The amateur liar usually has a poor memory, which is fatal to him. Often he is trapped when, after he has committed the perjury, he is led away from the subject only to be suddenly brought back again with a rude shock.

Names and numbers are particularly difficult to remember even when true, so that perjury concerning them is one of the easiest kinds detected. A rapid fire of questions, such as no mind can follow except that prompted by a truthful conscience, often displays willful falsehoods.

Falsehoods, when detected, are extremely detrimental

16

to the side which commits them. They discredit not only the particular testimony, but all thereafter introduced. Once a falsehood is detected, the trier of the facts believes many more are there which are still concealed. This destroys an otherwise just cause.

Some lawyers are gifted with an almost prophetic sense, because of the extremely high development of their intuitive faculties, whereby their intellect draws inferences quickly and sometimes almost instantaneously. They can usually cure perjury by using the sometime effective, but always dangerous double-edged sword—cross-examination.

The Object of Cross-Examination

❧❧

THE object of cross-examination is to test the truth of statements of a witness made on direct examination; to sift, modify, or explain what has been said; and to weaken or disprove the case of your adversary.

Cross-examination is the most potent weapon known to the law for separating falsehood from truth, hearsay from actual knowledge, things imaginary from things real, opinion from fact, and inference from recollection.

Good cross-examination is the result of thorough preparation and is most effective when based on knowledge of the legal and factual issues involved in a trial.

It is best not to cross-examine unless it is absolutely necessary or to ask a question unless the answer reasonably to be expected will aid your cause.

There is sound logic in this extreme position. A clear-cut, forceful answer given by a witness on cross-examination is more deadly in its effect on a jury than the same answer given on direct.

In a California courtroom not so many years ago a personal injury suit was in trial. The plaintiff contended he had been physically and financially injured as a result of an accident. He said so on the stand in a tone of voice calculated to arouse the sympathy of the jury.

The defendant was represented by an eager young practitioner who could hardly contain himself until the moment when he was able to begin questioning the plaintiff. The cross-examination went thusly:

Q. Did you, at the time of the accident, when you were asked if you were hurt, reply that you weren't hurt?
A. Yes, sir, I did.

The questioning should have gone no further. The plaintiff had admitted that at the time of the accident he said he had not been hurt. But our hero was not satisfied.

Q. Well, sir, why have you been testifying all morning that you were hurt, giving the jury the impression that you were still suffering the effects of the accident?
A. Well, Mr. Lawyer, it was like this. I was driving my horse and buggy along the road, and along comes this client of yours in his automobile and knocks us in the ditch. You never saw such a mess in all your life. I was flat on my back with my legs in the air. The buggy was completely wrecked. Now this client of yours gets out of his car and looks at us. He sees my horse has a broken leg. He goes back to his automobile, gets a gun, and shoots him. Then he comes up to me and says, "Now what about you? Are you hurt?"

Remember that the touchstone is always credibility; the ultimate measure of testimonial worth is quality and

19

not quantity. When you have gotten answers of quality, do not press for quantity. The road to losing a case is paved with the cobbles of frustration resulting from a desire for quantity.

There is nothing more dangerous than the cross-examination of what the law terms an expert witness, a person so qualified that his testimony is considered to be beyond question.

If expert testimony is expected, the cross-examiner must be sure he knows the subject. An expert should be employed and consulted in great detail while preparing the cross-examination. The expert should sit with the examiner during the direct and cross of the expert of the opposition. The good trial lawyer will not wade in blindly, and if he cannot master the subject, he will not cross-examine but will wait until he puts on his own expert.

The folly of tackling the testimony of an expert witness occurred in a drunk driving case. The arrest had been made by a police officer whose employment record showed the defense lawyer that he had been on the force only a short time. The cross-examination began:

Q. Patrolman Murphy, do you think that a year's experience as a police officer qualifies you to state that my client was intoxicated?

A. No, sir.

Q. Upon what, then, do you base your statement that my client was drunk?

A. Fourteen years of bartending.

Honest opinions of different experts can be obtained on opposite sides of the same question, and dishonest opinions may be obtained on different sides of the same question. There is distinction between scientific facts and of opinions. Medical experts may be called to establish medical facts which are not matters of opinion. On such facts the experts will not disagree, but in the field of opinion, experts differ widely among themselves.

A person is qualified to testify as an expert if he has special knowledge, skill, experience, training, or education sufficient to qualify him as an expert on the subject to which his testimony relates.

A duly qualified expert may give his opinions on questions in controversy at a trial. The jury may consider the expert's opinion with the reasons given for it, if any. It may also consider the qualifications and credibility of the expert; it is not bound to accept an expert opinion as conclusive but should give to it the weight to which it finds it to be entitled. Also, it may disregard any such opinion if it finds it unreasonable.

In examining an expert witness, counsel may propound to him a type of question known in the law as a hypothetical question. By such a question the witness is asked to assume to be true a hypothetical state of facts and to give an opinion based on that assumption.

In permitting such a question, the court does not rule and does not necessarily find that all the assumed facts have been proved. It only determines that those assumed facts are within the probable or possible range of the

21

evidence. It is for the jury to find from all the evidence whether or not the facts assumed in a hypothetical question have been proved, and if it should find that any assumption in such a question has not been proved, it is to determine the effect of that failure of proof on the value and weight of the expert opinion based on the content of the hypothetical question.

Many lawyers try to cope with a medical expert on his own ground. In rare instances this is productive of satisfactory results. It affords an opportunity for the doctor to enlarge on the testimony he has already given and to explain what might otherwise have been misunderstood or even entirely overlooked.

Careful and judicious questions, seeking to bring out the separate facts and separate points from the knowledge and experience of the expert, which tend to support the theory of the trial lawyer's side of the case, produce good results.

The effect of the testimony of an expert witness may sometimes be destroyed by putting the witness to some unexpected and offhand test at the trial, in reference to his experience, his ability and discrimination as an expert, so that in case of his failure to meet the test, he can be held up to ridicule before the jury.

It frequently happens that the expert (the physician) has never seen or examined the patient concerning whose condition he is giving sworn testimony in response to a prepared hypothetical question. Juries will accept the answer of the witness as direct evidence of the existence

22

of the fact itself. These hypothetical questions are usually loosely and inaccurately framed and present a very different aspect of the case from that which the testimony of the witnesses would justify.

It is possible for the trial lawyer to demolish the damaging effect of the hypothetical question. One method is to ask the physician that he repeat, in substance, the question that had just been put to him and on which he bases his answer. The stumbling effort of the witness to recall the various stages of the question points up to the jury the dangers of such testimony.

Some experts, before being sworn as witnesses, study the typewritten hypothetical question which they are to answer. One question will develop the course to follow. If the witness answers that he has previously read the question, ask him which particular part of it he lays the most stress on and which parts he could throw out. You may gradually narrow him down to some factor in the hypothetical question the truth of which the previous testimony in the case might have left in doubt.

Hypothetical questions do not, of course, include facts which might develop later for the defense. When cross-examining, therefore, it is often useful to inquire in what respect the witness would modify his answer if he were to assume the truth of these new factors in the case.

Some lawyers write down the questions to be asked, but the experienced trial lawyer will not do so. Reading them will cause the examiner to miss the reactions of the witness, and he will find himself paying more attention to reading the next question than listening to the answer to the former.

In preparation for extended cross-examination, outlines should be made which contain appropriate headings, as well as notations of documents available or other evidence in the examiner's possession. Often such outlines are altered by the testimony as it unfolds, but these outlines will be a checklist so that nothing important will be overlooked.

If no daily transcript of the testimony is available, then some notes should be taken during the direct examination. The examiner must decide whether taking notes diverts his attention from the witness or from objecting to questions.

Above all, the cross-examiner must concentrate on the witness: on the way he is answering questions and on his effect on the judge and jury.

In cross-examination, loaded or leading questions may be asked. A witness may be confronted with a fact to which he has not testified, or he may be confronted by a contrary statement which he is purported to have made at another time.

But when a new fact is injected into a question on cross-examination, the examiner must be prepared to follow it up with proof during the course of his case.

It is good practice to start questioning without hesitation. The initial question need not necessarily concern a basic proposition; it should be clear, sharp, and asked promptly.

But the most important decision is whether to cross-examine at all.

No matter how long the witness has taken on direct, if his testimony has done no harm, then there is no need to cross-examine, even though the witness can be confronted with certain misstatements. If the witness has done some slight harm, it is safer to introduce contradictory testimony than to cross-examine.

Suppose the opposite has occurred—the witness, who has testified to matters which are definitely harmful, appears to be strong, vigorous, and with definite convictions, while the examiner has no contradictory proof available to assist in the cross-examination. Then the most that ought to be done is to ask some minor or collateral questions and drop the witness.

To illustrate: If he is a medical witness, he should be asked who employed him, how much he is being paid, how many times he examined the litigant, and whether he examined him for the purpose of testifying or for treatment.

It is wise to pick out one or two salient points concerning which the examiner thinks he can discredit the witness rather than to review everything in detail. If this course succeeds, it can be argued to the jury that if he erred in part, he erred in whole.

Determine before starting to cross-examine whether the purpose is to discredit or to destroy the witness. At times both will be accomplished, but the two objectives are different.

Discrediting a witness means generally that by reason of his faulty observation or failure to recall a matter after a considerable period of time, his testimony does not accurately present the facts.

It is often essential to show the state of feeling of a witness for the purpose of giving the jury all the facts necessary to a full and fair consideration of his testimony and determination of the credit to be given to it.

He may be discredited by showing his bias, as by evidence of near relationship to a party, sympathy, hostility, or prejudice, and this may be done by his own testimony or by other evidence.

He may be impeached by extrinsic evidence showing bias or hostility toward the party against whom he testifies. It is generally necessary, at least where the extrinsic evidence consists of previous statements of the witness, to lay the same foundation as is necessary for impeachment by prior inconsistent statements.

For example: If the witness has identified the cross-examiner's client, then he should be questioned concerning clothing or other identification marks to determine what basis he had for making his identification.

A prepared checklist of the various questions to be asked concerning identification should be adhered to and the witness taken over every item. This must be done with great calm and apparent unconcern.

To discredit the witness further, any inadequacy of his perceptive faculties should be brought out: inaccurate recollection; tendency to exaggerate; unsoundness of judgment of time and distance; and the inherent improbability of the truth of all or portions of his direct testimony.

To destroy the witness, it is necessary to show his interest, direct or indirect, in the outcome of the litigation; his motives; his relationship to or association with the party calling him; his friendship, hostility, bias, or prejudice; his improper conduct in the case, such as attempting to influence other witnesses; or his conviction of a crime rendering him unworthy of belief.

Interest creates a motive for false testimony; the greater the interest, the stronger is the temptation. Witnesses, whose memories are prodded by the eagerness of interested parties to elicit testimony favorable to themselves, are not usually to be depended on for accurate information.

If the witness appears strong or firm or vigorous, it is best to attack indirectly. Suppose a witness testifies to a particular conversation and there is no indication that the witness did not have a distinct recollection of the conversation; then he should not be questioned concerning it at the start. Instead, he should be asked when he was first informed that he would be a witness, what subject matter was reviewed, what questions were asked, and who was present.

Surprisingly this line of questions often confuses the witness; he will be concerned about disclosing his conference with the other attorney prior to taking the stand; he will hesitate in answering, will contradict himself frequently on these unimportant matters, and thus will cast grave doubt on the substantive part of his testimony.

When a witness seems to be mechanically reciting his testimony, the best cross-examination is to secure repetition of the same subject, but not immediately. He should be led over some of the ground and then adroitly asked a question which produces the same answer. If the witness has been coached, such tactics are usually effective and productive.

The good trial lawyer will set the pace of the questions and the changes of subject matter. The deliberateness of a particular witness may be emphasized by permitting him to take his time in answering the questions. Occasionally the question "Well, can we have the answer now?" or "Have you decided what the answer is?" points out to the jury that the witness is taking too much time to make up his mind, the inference being that he is not sure of the facts.

Some witnesses are very skillful in rephrasing the question before answering. Therefore, questions should be framed so that they can be answered yes or no. The witness must not be permitted to phrase the question the way he desires and then to answer it. He should be pinned down and kept there.

The cross-examiner will never use violent or abusive language to a witness, nor will he browbeat or bulldoze him or coerce or approach the witness so closely as to embarrass or intimidate him. This does not mean that the witness need be shielded against embarrassment resulting from proper cross-examination.

Questions asked of a witness on cross-examination must be definite, certain, and not argumentative.

It is a must that the examiner maintain a serene appearance during cross-examination. There must be no evidence of satisfaction or dissatisfaction. If a critical question is asked, the answer to which is detrimental, another question should be asked immediately. Thus, even though the answer is harmful, its full effect may not be apparent.

Cross-examination should not be overdone and should stop when the witness has given a beneficial answer. If it is in the record once, then it can be used with determination. The danger in pursuing the same inquiry is that ofttimes the witness is permitted to get off the hook; a second thought occurs to him, or there is a recess and somebody calls his attention to what he has forgotten.

Cross-examination which follows literally the order of the direct is least calculated to produce a satisfactory result. The witness, through pretrial preparation and direct examination, has learned this sequence and is usually ready with his answer before the cross-examiner's question is finished.

Neither is it ordinarily good tactics to commence a cross-examination with the subject matter last testified to on direct. This is fresh in the mind of the witness, and he is not likely to contradict it if immediately cross-examined on it. But when the cross-examiner has in his hands convincing impeachment on the subject, he should

29

immediately put the impeaching matter to the witness in a series of crisp, rapid questions. This tactic may be so disconcerting that it will throw him completely off-balance during the remainder of the cross-examination.

Many different types appear as witnesses:

There is the essentially honest witness who, because of his partisanship, has gone further than the facts warrant.

There is the belligerent witness, who, because of relationship, interest, prejudice, or other antagonism, is determined to assist to the limit of his capacity the party who calls him.

There is the smart-aleck witness, given to wisecracks, who believes he is a match for any lawyer.

There is the timid, hesitant witness, about whom the lawyer must determine quickly whether the hesitation is due to uncertainty on the facts or to a natural disposition.

There is the ignorant witness, whose perceptive faculties are none too good and who has been persuaded into giving favorable direct testimony to facts of which he has no actual knowledge.

There is the evasive or reluctant witness, whose attitude suggests the concealment of facts which would weaken the direct testimony he has given.

There is the artful witness, who has cleverly woven a harmful lie into a fabric of other testimony admittedly true.

Finally, there is the vicious, reckless witness, who has willfully sworn falsely.

In each of these cases the style of cross-examination will necessarily depend on the lawyer's natural disposition. Speaking generally, there are two prevailing styles: the savage, slashing, hammer-and-tongs method of going after a witness to make him tell the truth; and the smiling, soft-spoken, ingratiating method, directed to lulling the witness into a sense of security and gaining his confidence. Neither style can be adopted to the exclusion of the other.

Experience has taught that the gentler approach is best. The savage, vehement style of cross-examination ordinarily makes the hostile witness more hostile. In some instances such an examination angers the witness to the point of impelling him to give vicious answers.

While this result may weaken the effect of his direct testimony by emphasizing his partisanship and hostility, the content of the answer may be such as to lead the jury to believe that the witness is beating the examiner at his own game.

If a witness is caught in inconsistencies, the slashing, bulldozing type of examination may add to the witness' confusion, but the soft-spoken type will usually get the witness to talk volubly, and his effort to reconcile the inconsistencies usually emphasizes them.

Whenever the witness is apparently honest and has tried to give his best recollection of an occurrence, any cross-examination undertaken should be pursued only to the point of obtaining some favorable limitation of, or addition to, his direct testimony. Then he should be dismissed with an air suggesting that his entire testimony lacks importance.

The determination of when to end a cross-examination is more important than when to begin it. If possible, end on a high note. Drop the witness after a telling point has been scored. The legitimate advantages of a brilliant cross-examination are thrown away by an interrogation on petty or immaterial details.

Great examiners have in the first instance been greater lawyers. There have been no great cross-examiners who have not been great lawyers. By experience, by training, by development of technique, by participating in trials, the lawyer develops an instinctive ability to do the right thing at the right time.

Mental Functions of the Witness

MENTAL functions are connected with and dependent on the body, and they cannot operate normally if the physical man is ill or is deficient. The mind depends on the action of the brain. Experience and experimentation have established that destruction of the brain or its impairment causes a corresponding affectation of the mind to all visible extents.

The main parts of the body on which the brain depends are the various sense organs: the eyes, ears, nose, mouth, and skin. They are the receiving apparatus for the brain, and all acts and conscious processes are initiated by stimulation of the senses. If these are abnormal in any respect, whether through injury or disease, the mind cannot function normally. It cannot receive a normal impulse from the affected sense organ, nor can it transmit a normal impulse to an affected organ.

Physical weakness handicaps a witness and frequently lessens his ability to give accurate and complete testimony. The trial lawyer must be careful in observing the physical limits of the witness, but it should be done before the trial if possible.

The character of the testimony depends on the mental ability of the witness to observe, to comprehend, to remember, and to express facts. If any one of these factors is influenced in a detrimental way by a physical deficiency, the evidence is nearly always inaccurate.

People vary in the sensitiveness of their perceptions. People vary in the clearness with which they see. Lack of capacity to distinguish colors from one another is common. Color blindness as a pathological fact is well known, but it is not widely understood that between normal vision for colors and pathological color blindness there are numerous stages of defect which render people insensitive to many niceties of hue and shade.

In hearing, we know that elderly people are less acute than children and that there is wide variation in the keenness of hearing of different individuals. A similar distinction marks the capacity of different people to distinguish notes of different pitch and tone.

Assume the apocryphal damage case against a railroad for personal injuries sustained, in which it is claimed that the defendant's locomotive did not sound its whistle as it approached a crossing. A witness who could scarcely hear would be of little or no value. Or the case rests on whether a red or green light was displayed. It would be disastrous to rely on a witness whose color blindness was disclosed by your opponent in cross-examination.

But a witness who has the necessary physical qualifications must also have powers: (1) of perception; (2) of memory; and (3) of expression.

Perception includes observation and comprehension. It is the process by which facts are realized by the mind so that there they may be remembered and reproduced. When a stimulus is presented to the senses, we are merely aware of it without understanding it; we have sensation, but not perception. But if that awareness has delineation, comprehension, and recognition, then we have perception. Unless there is accurate perception, the desired facts may never have been understood by the witness, thus resulting in distorted evidence.

Attention is the necessary factor for accurate and complete perception. Accurate attention is beyond the power of most people. Witnesses will not agree on all essential particulars. One person will see or hear the situation from one angle, while another will see or hear it from a different angle.

Attention is giving heed to some impression which is asking the consciousness for recognition. It is a channel through which perception may take place and without which perception cannot take place.

The observation on which most evidence is based results from very casual attention. Seldom is there any knowledge at the time the situation is witnessed that the person will be called upon months or years later to testify under oath in court about what happened. Witnesses usually make no attempt to remember carefully until they receive subpoenas to appear in court.

In addition to attention, the range of observation or perception depends on the quickness of assimilation and retentiveness.

A witness must understand what he is seeing or hearing. Without this knowledge he cannot understand what is taking place, cannot remember it, and cannot testify to what occurred. To illustrate: Two men, four blocks away, were engaged in a street fight. The witness could testify to the blows struck, but when it came to what words passed between the combatants during the fight, he would be incapacitated because he did not hear the words used.

In weighing the reliability of the testimony, we must consider the ability of the witness to perceive the facts as regards attention and as regards the manner in which the facts were connected in his mind.

Inaccuracies of perception are: (1) insufficient attention; (2) meagerness of experiences for use in association; (3) low mental retentiveness; (4) faint imagery in terms of which to picture the objects; (5) lack of conscientiousness in keeping apart that which is observed and that which is inferred; and (6) the effect of suggestion by which other ideas may be fitted into the story.

Memory is a reinstatement of an old experience or a present consciousness of an old experience. Probably the largest number of errors in testimony are caused by faulty memory, because the testimony of witnesses, with few exceptions, is based on mere incidental memory. Many people make no effort to remember what happened, and if called to testify later, they have probably forgotten much of what they originally perceived.

Memory depends on two main factors: one, the fact that whenever a fact is perceived, there is formed in the brain certain pathways, and the longer the plasticity of the brain allows these paths to remain, the longer and better the memory; and two, not only the degree to which the original facts were perceived but how well they were learned and fixed in the mind.

Recall is beyond our control. It is dependent on the associations that were established at the moment of learning. A person recalls if he has established a connection between an event and a bit of knowledge. If the association has not been established, the knowledge, even if possessed, is not aroused, and it is as if it had never been known.

When the trial lawyer asks a question, there arises in the mind of the witness all those bits of knowledge which are associated in his mind with the subject of the question. Recall takes place, and the witness answers the question.

Time is the essence of memory. The greater the elapsed time between observing an event and testifying on it in court, the greater will be the unreliability of the testimony. The memory of everyone is subject to deterioration.

Forgetting or normal weakness of memory is not of so great an importance to the trial lawyer as are illusions of memory, which are frequent, subtle, and difficult to detect.

37

Memory illusion consists in the illusory opinion of having experienced, seen, or heard something, although there has been no such experience, seeing, or hearing. It is difficult to discover or perceive because it enters unobtrusively and unnoticed into the circle of observation, and not directly by means of a demonstrated mistake.

It is well recognized that a person may remember facts and situations which never happened to him at all. In such a case the facts have been supplied by the imagination or by suggestion.

Suggestion creates artificial memory out of nothing and changes existing memories to suit its own ends. It is one of the principal causes of inaccurate testimony. Newspapers are very suggestive. That is one reason why witnesses should always be asked whether they have been reading accounts of the event about which they are asked to testify. It is safe to conclude that the memory of the witness will be tainted with suggestive influences if he has been reading the papers which have been playing up the event.

A friendly witness is a fertile field for sowing the seeds of suggestion, and it is not difficult to take a child and so suggestively to fix him that he will testify to facts which he says he remembers but which were implanted in his memory by suggestion.

Memory may be altered by constant talking about the facts remembered. Each time the event is discussed the exact truth is varied slightly. After much talk the event may lose all resemblance to its original form. No better illustration can be found of this weakness than in the way rumor travels from lip to lip, starting from some small insignificant fact and ending in a mountain of scandal.

When the trial lawyer thinks that the memory of the witness has become perverted through much talking, he should cross-examine carefully to determine just how much talking there has been: how many times has the witness told the story and how many people have listened to it.

Many people think that the correct recall of one feature of an event makes certain that other features of the same event are also being correctly recalled. This is not the case. Correct recall of one part of a situation does not guarantee the correctness of recollections of other parts of the same situation, even though there is logical connection between the facts recalled.

Another mental qualification which a witness must possess is the power of expression. No matter how accurate the observation, how clear the comprehension, or how enduring the memory, the testimony is without value unless the witness can express his thoughts in words.

Words are the main vehicles of expression. The witness who uses forceful and plausible words is much better than one who does not. The trial lawyer must evaluate the power of expression of a witness. Where any one of several witnesses may be used, the power of expression should be the guide to a choice between them.

Frailty of Human Testimony

❧❧❧

It is perplexing and seemingly inexplicable to hear honest and intelligent men and women array themselves on opposite sides of a case and testify under oath to what appears to be absolutely contradictory statements of fact.

Trial lawyers and judges know that human testimony is largely the product of inaccurate observation, distorted recollection, baseless inferences, and conjecture.

The trial lawyer must demonstrate the emptiness of vague conjecture and the shakiness of a scaffolding erected almost exclusively on guesswork, probability, and presumption.

When an honest witness testifies to something he saw or heard, he represents that he accurately saw or heard some past event, that he accurately remembers what he saw or heard, and that now, in the courtroom, he is accurately reporting his memory.

His testimony is a report of his beliefs resulting from his reaction to an event. Observation and memory are not mechanical processes. An eyewitness does not necessarily reproduce sights and sounds accurately.

Part of what we see comes from the object before us. Another part (and it may be the larger part) always comes from our minds.

We fill in gaps in our observations. We interpolate, with unconscious imagination, things we did not observe. We fill in what is but a bare outline so as to meet what our past experience leads us to expect. We are frequently governed by our wishes.

We see what we want to see. We are apt to see what we expect—or wish or fear—to see and overlook what we are inclined to disbelieve.

Seeing is a complex affair; it is mingled with inferences, judgments, interpretations. All observation involves some unconscious inferences; consequently, there is a mixture of observation, inference, and imagination.

Much evidence introduced in court about threats or other spoken words is the witness describing not the language which operated on his senses, but the conclusions he formed from hearing them.

Many witnesses, because of bad eyesight, give inaccurate testimony about a crime or its perpetrator. Army and Navy tests and tests for applicants for driver's licenses disclose that a large number of Americans see inadequately. When men grow older, they become nearsighted or farsighted. A color-blind witness will mistake the color of a man's hair or of his suit.

Compare the momentary observation of a witness with

that of a physicist conducting an experiment in a laboratory. The physicist meticulously records what he sees the moment after he sees it.

Unlike the scientist, a witness of a robbery or a murder engages in no carefully prepared observation. Usually he does not immediately record his observation, nor has he concentrated his attention on what happened.

Other factors may cause his inattention. He may be fatigued, or he may be drunk, or a headache may distract him, or he may have business worries, or he may be frightened.

A partly deaf person may not hear a shot or, having heard it, may misjudge the direction from which it came, but the hunter is sensitive to the sound of a shot. A garage mechanic will hear or see defects under the hood of a car that the owner does not notice. A policeman's view of a burglarized house may differ from that of its owner.

Details of a transaction described by a variety of witnesses, each relating incidents which especially attracted his attention, show each believing he is right and the others are wrong.

Inadequate attention induces misinterpretations of what is actually seen, so testimony about a man's size may depend on whether the witness saw him lying on the ground or standing.

There is a tendency to overestimate the size of an empty room or an empty lot and to underestimate the size of a small person in the company of a larger one.

Most people are from time to time subject to illusions.

There are times when we seem to see or hear something real that in fact does not exist. Fatigue, overeating, hunger, loss of blood, fever, drugs, or fear may cause such imaginings. Illusions and hallucinations color observations and often produce false testimony.

Each witness dwells partly in a world of his own. He sees in terms of his needs, personality, temperament, emotions. Each interprets what he sees in his own fashion.

Physiologically, the so-called average man or the normal man is a fiction. People live in different worlds so far as their sensory reactions are concerned. Sight sensations, hearing sensations, and smell sensations differ. Every person has a pattern of existence distinctively different from all others.

Mistakes of memory are dangerously present if the witness must recollect his perception after a long time. Memory does not mirror the past; memory re-creates the past.

Although the workings of memory have been studied for centuries, they remain a mystery. Just how and why we remember, just how and why we forget, no one can completely explain.

What a witness remembers, how long he remembers, and the conditions that cause him to recall what he remembers—all depend on his own peculiar internal factors. They include his inherited abilities, his unique life experiences. Some have exceptional memories of sounds; others of color or touch or taste.

Psychologists think that forgetting is a fading or decaying of memory owing to the lapse of time. New events interfere or obliterate recollection of the old. In this prosess, each man's individuality influences his rate of forgetting past incidents.

The most frequent cause of false memory consists of the accounts we give others of our experience. We usually make such accounts simpler and more interesting than the truth. We quote what we should have said or done rather than what we really said or did. In the first telling we may be fully aware of the distinction, but as time pases, the fiction replaces reality in our memory.

Pride colors memory. " 'I have done that,' says my memory. 'I cannot have done that,' says my pride." Finally my memory yields.

Pride also plays an important part in trials. The district attorney asks the witness about a purse snatching in his presence eight months ago. Actually the witness was not very attentive at the time; he was thinking of raising money to refinance his home mortgage. But in court he thinks he remembers the details of the purse snatching. The witness identifies the suspect as the man who did it, and he so testifies.

On cross-examination, defense counsel challenges his memory. This challenge makes the witness angry. He resents any doubts about his memory. The more the cross-examiner tries, the more stubborn the witness becomes; the more certain he is that he is right.

Judicial comments by experienced trial judges show that witnesses persuade themselves that they remember bygone circumstances which never occurred and that it is common for an honest witness to confuse what he actually saw with what he has persuaded himself he saw.

There is danger that a conscientious person, in trying to narrate the transaction which exists in his memory in a faded or fragmentary state, will, in his effort to make the reproduction complete and natural, substitute fancy for fact or fabricate the missing or forgotten links.

Lawyers have wide latitude in cross-examining an adverse witness in an effort to show that he is prejudiced for the side that called him.

Prejudice colors a witness' memory. Even witnesses who are upright and honest are apt to be more or less warped by their partiality or prejudice for or against one of the parties.

Often the prejudices of an honest witness are unconscious. Without being aware of it, he may be hostile. Such concealed prejudice, unknown to the witness or anyone else, may be the cause of the gravest mistakes in his testimony. His buried unconscious animosity toward one of the litigants may distort the facts of a robbery he saw or may mistakenly identify the accused as the man charged with murder.

The witness sees a fight between the police and union pickets. His original impression is confused. If he is an ardent union sympathizer, he may later remember with clarity that the police brutally assaulted the pickets.

Witnesses usually feel complimented by the confidence of the party calling them to prove a certain state of facts.

They do not deliberately falsify to please the caller, but the desire to be an important element in the case is uppermost in their minds. Biased witnesses are much addicted to half-truths and are more dangerous than those who commit perjury.

A trial is a process of communication between witnesses and jurors. No matter how accurate a witness' observation and memory, his testimony will mislead the jury if the jury misunderstands what he says. The meaning of a word is not in the word only, but in the way it is used. There are illusion and erroneous assumption that we invariably know what others mean.

We judge the truth of what a man says to us by the way he says it: "He looked me square in the eye" or "He had a shifty gaze." The demeanor of a witness while testifying in the courtroom is of primary importance: his gestures; grimaces, intonations; his straightforward or evasive manner; his facial expressions; his hesitations; his fluency.

Every trial lawyer knows that the jury gives close attention to the manner of witnesses while testifying and are sometimes more strongly influenced by appearances than they are by the words of the witnesses. A juror can see, as well as hear, and the juror's eyes and ears aid in making up his mind about what weight shall be given to the evidence of a witness.

Although the demeanor of the witness often helps illuminate the truth or falsity of testimony, it may do just the opposite. An unscrupulous lying witness, well trained, may not betray himself by his manner. He may look the jury square in the eye; he may have an excellent poker face.

And an honest witness may so behave as to arouse the jury's distrust. He may have an unpleasant, squeaky voice or a habit of twisting his fingers. He may be restless, peevish, or he may talk in a sneering manner. If he is nervous and timid, he may seem furtive and evasive.

No sooner are his ideas uttered than he becomes conscious of errors. If he attempts an explanation, it usually results in his discomfiture. If he should persist in misrepresentation or concealment, a new cause of embarrassment arises in the fear of subsequent exposure and leads to still more harmful falsehoods and suppressions.

Ofttimes a witness leads the jury to suspect that he is lying because he has too strong a sense of the proprieties of his position as a witness to resent a suggestion of untruthfulness when cross-examined.

A disturbed neurotic may appear to be a serene and accurate witness, at worst only an eccentric, but his hidden subjective fears and anxieties, unrelated to the external situation, may interfere with his capacity to perceive or recollect accurately.

An aged and dignified witness may suffer lapses of memory which he cleverly conceals, even from himself, filling in the gaps with falsities, but he may impress a jury. Again there are witnesses, young in years, afflicted with premature senility, who have similar difficulties which they similarly conceal.

The numberless errors in perceptions derived from the senses, the faults of memory, the differences in human beings as regards sex, nature, culture, moods of the moment, health, passionate excitement, environment—all these things have so great an effect that we scarcely ever receive two similar accounts of one thing.

Witnesses, speaking of the same incident, will characterize it as a very ordinary event or altogether a joke or quite disgusting. Now it is possible to think that people who have so variously characterized the same event will give an identical description of the act. But they have seen the event with their own eyes. One has seen nothing, another something else, and although the seeing may have lasted only a few moments, each has in mind a personally attuned picture which he now reproduces.

One man overlooks half because he is not looking at the right place, another substitutes his inferences, and another seeks to rationalize what he has seen.

To tell the truth implies accurate observation, knowledge of the importance of facts, and the power of description. A man's power to speak the truth depends on his knowledge and his form of expression. His knowledge depends on his accuracy of observation, his memory, and his presence of mind.

A stool pigeon's testimony is always dangerous. Jurors are impressed by such testimony. They believe that the confessing accomplice tells the truth in order to clear his own conscience.

The prosecution frequently assures an accomplice that

he will not be prosecuted if he gives testimony against the accused. This is buying perjury.

Jurors are witnesses of what goes on at the trial. They must determine the facts of the case from the words and demeanor of the testifying witnesses.

Jurors make mistakes similar to those of the testifying witnesses: They may misunderstand or forget some of the testimony. Some jurors may have defective hearing; they may miss or misunderstand testimony. Similarly, a juror's defective eyesight may interfere with his observation of an important witness' demeanor.

Trial lawyers are familiar with the recurring spectacle of lawyers and judges disagreeing on what testimony has been given by a witness a short time before. Thus, even men of trained minds, whose special attention is on the witness, who realize the importance of every word, may receive inconsistent impressions of his testimony.

Like testifying witnesses, jurors may have conscious or unconscious prejudices. They may be biased against a litigant or against some of his witnesses. These prejudices may lead a jury to an erroneous judgment.

People think that a trial is a courtroom investigation of all the available evidence, an investigation so conducted that it will enable the jury to ascertain the truth. This is not the case. The legal profession's current conception of a fair trial is a battle between lawyers according to certain legally established ground rules, enforced by the judge, with the jury deciding the winner.

Many believe that this fighting method brings out the

truth and that the best way for a jury to learn the facts is to have the lawyer for each side direct the jury's attention to the evidence favorable to his side and to discredit the evidence introduced by the opposition.

Lawyers praise the fighting-trial method as the best way to find the actual facts, but the same lawyers express admiration for the members of their profession who are most adept at the manipulation of courtroom procedures for the obfuscation of issues and the confusion of juries.

Under the concept that a trial is a fight, the legal profession endorses as wholly reputable some tactics that do not encourage an accurate determination of the facts. You will find those wiles and tricks explained in dozens of books on trial techniques designed for other lawyers— not the general public who make up our juries.

These books advise the lawyer that he has a duty to give the jury, if possible, a false impression of testimony unfavorable to his side, and if an honest witness is timid, the lawyer should, by cross-examination, play up that weakness in order to persuade the jury that the witness is concealing important facts.

To tangle up most witnesses by such means is fairly easy. The role of witness represents a frightening experience for the ordinary honest person. The novelty of the situation, the agitation and hurry which accompany it, the cajolery or intimidation to which the witness is subjected, and the confusion of cross-examination may give rise to important errors and omissions.

What the Witness Saw and Heard

CROSS-EXAMINATION is the fierce wildcat of the courtroom, and dangerous too.

The defendant in a criminal action is all too often "up for grabs." The state and its functionaries claim he is guilty of some offense. While the prosecution must prove the charge to a moral certainty and beyond a reasonable doubt, Mr. Do-right, who reads the newspapers, smacks his lips and gloats each time the state shovels another wretch into a criminal court. "Got to be guilty," says he; "wouldn't be there in the first place if they didn't have the right man."

Trying a case—standing on your feet and searching your brain for quick answers—is a heady wine for the best man; the slow thinker may soon have a dead client.

The truth of the testimony of witnesses against the defendant is something in which too many people place too much faith. Most witnesses do not lie, but they are open to suggestion and sometimes say anything that the prose-

51

cutor puts in their minds. Lawyers too are poor witnesses in court; experience with people in litigation has made them much more aware than other people that man's perceptive powers are unreliable. Cross-examination has proved that no two persons perceive the same event with the same set of eyes.

Many factors influence a witness. Studies made by psychologists tend to prove that a person's feelings, suggestions, emotions, empathy, association influence the witness' capacity for accurate, objective perception. And because we have few tests at the early stage of a trial to determine a witness's reliability, an innocent man may be sent to the penitentiary by an honest but completely biased witness.

The history of placing the witness' credibility under scrutiny dates as far back as the fourteenth century. During the 1300's, judges maintained that the indispensable requisite to forming an opinion on the trustworthiness of a witness was that the witness appear personally before the judge. The court could then gain certain impressions of the witness' manner of answering questions, his reactions, behavior, and physical appearance.

Following the examination, the judge would then put into the record his reactions to the witness: that the witness stammered or hesitated in replying to specific questions or showed fear during the examination, as well as any other impressions of the witness and his testimony that the judge felt impelled to record.

The natural and acquired shrewdness and experience

by which an observant judge or juror forms an opinion on whether a witness is lying or telling the truth are by far the most important of all their qualifications, infinitely more important than any acquaintance with the law.

Insofar as the judge's or juror's abilities to perceive truth, falsehood, or simply added confusion in a witness are concerned, no school of law, no set of books, will qualify him. Such knowledge can be gained only by experience. Here the juror may be handicapped since he has probably had little of it in this most subtle art of all: detection and preservation of the truth when dealing with a witness.

People come before a jury with their cases prepared and give evidence which they have determined they will give. Like untidy housekeepers, many people come before the judge and jury with clean floors; all the dirt is hidden under the rug. It is necessary to do a little rug lifting, if the truth is to be found.

The observations of witnesses are either generalities too vague to be of much practical use or so narrow and special that they can be diagnosed only by personal observation and practical experience. The most acute observer would never be able to catalogue the myriad tones of voice, the passing shades of expression, or the unconscious gestures which he has by tradition learned to associate with falsehood. And this is the plight of the cross-examiner standing before jurors who have limited experience in matters of ascertaining the truthfulness of a witness.

The English and American traditional procedures of examination are doubtless entitled to high praise. It is the rarest and highest personal accomplishment of a judge or juror to make allowance for the ignorance and timidity of witnesses and to be able to see clearly through the confident and plausible liar.

Our courtroom procedure vests the jury with immense power, not always subject to correction when the case may be appealed. The jury's estimate of the credibility of a witness may frequently stem from an absurd rule of thumb: the assumption that when a witness wipes his hands profusely during his testimony, he is lying. But unless the judge somehow reveals in the trial record that he or the jury used such an irrational method of determining credibility, the higher courts can do nothing to correct the error; they will have to assume that the judge or jury used some infallible system, not governed by human vagaries.

To understand better why trial lawyers—who love the law but are still driven to despair by some of its facets—sometimes have sour dispositions, let us examine what actually happens when oral testimony is being heard by a judge and jury.

When an honest witness testifies to something he saw, he represents that he accurately saw or heard something of importance to the case, which now in the courtroom he accurately remembers to the most finite detail. Our witness would like us to believe he is a combination movie camera and tape recorder.

Insofar as his initial observation of the event, his memory of the observation of that event (for some time has now passed between the event and the trial), and his verbal communication in the courtroom are concerned, error can enter—and often does.

Judge Jerome Frank in his learned writings contends that when a witness says: "I say" or "I heard" what he really means it: "I believe I saw" or "I think I heard." His testimony consists of nothing but a report of his beliefs, and this report is not a documented series of facts, just a series of moldy recollections that have been colored by the passage of time and by the talks he may have had with the district attorney or the police.

William James best expressed the state of mind of the average witness when he said: "Whilst part of what we perceive comes from the object before us, another part (and it may be the larger part) always comes out of our mind."

Judges and jurors also fulfill the function of a witness —a witness to what goes on during the trial. They must decide the facts of the case from what they see and hear —that is, from the words, as well as from the demeanor, of the testifying witnesses.

Reduced to absolutes, the judge and the jury are witnesses of the witnesses, and if those who testify are not to be likened to scientific observers, neither are the judges or the jurors: They make the same mistakes the testifying witnesses make.

If a judge or a juror has a hearing defect, he is bound

to miss some important point or misunderstand the testimony. The communication process between a key witness and a partially deaf (or dozing) judge or juror may be likened to a conversation that takes place between a Swahili and a Swede: Little, if anything, will get through. Similarly, defective eyesight may interfere with the juror's observation of an important witness' demeanor, such as a prosecution witness testifying against the defendant with a smirk on his face.

Deficient memory of the testimony that has been given in the courtroom will surely lead to error later in the jury room. And don't believe that because twelve jurors have heard the same testimony, the majority will necessarily have understood it. Usually, it is the mistaken juror whose bray will eventually bring the others around.

To evaluate the reliability of a witness' testimony would in most instances require a knowledge of his personality. Men's minds are modified by the influence of their environment or by the way their passions and sentiments are involved: how they love or hate; how they struggle in every sphere of society; and how their social, pecuniary, family, or political interests might clash.

The best cure for these legal and mental inequities would simply be that more people be aware of the frailties and unreliabilities of man's so-called powers of perception. Since we know how unreliable the best can be when it comes to memory, it would be better that all of us be tolerant of honest mistakes. No man who is honest with himself can ever stand pat on the accuracy of his own testimony. He not only may be mistaken, but often is.

In his historic work on evidence, Simon Greenleaf writes that cross-examination is one of the most efficacious tests which the law has devised for the discovery of truth, its object being that the judge or jury, by this opportunity of observing a witness' demeanor and of determining the just weight and value of his testimony, may better understand the character of the witness it is called on to believe; his situation with respect to the parties and to the subject of litigation; his interest, motives, inclination, and prejudices; his means of correct and certain knowledge of the facts.

The problem of truth and the search for the accurate, truthful witness is, has been, and will always be the endless occupation of the good cross-examiner.

It is a fascinating search, for it may lead into the strangest lands and onto the most distant shores of human experience. And because the truth is purely a human experience, it has within it all of man's faults and virtues.

The Eyewitness

EVERY year the following scene, with modifications, will be played out in one of our universities.

Some twenty students sit in a classroom, their heads bent over examination papers. Suddenly the door pops open, and a young woman, about five feet tall and dressed in levis, a plaid hunting shirt, and a green Tyrolean hat, bursts into the room. She quickly levels a carrot at a student seated in the first row and shouts: "Federal herring! You stole my marks!" Outside, in the corridor, a popping sound is heard.

A student in the front row clutches his breast, screams, and falls to the floor. As the assailant runs out, two men dressed as ambulance attendants enter the room, drag the victim to his feet, and quickly carry him away.

The whole scene has taken almost one minute from the time the assailant enters until the victim is removed.

When the class has quieted down, the instructor rises to his feet and says: "Ladies and gentlemen, I want all of you to take a fresh sheet of paper and describe *everything* that just took place in this room. Tell me exactly what happened and give a complete physical description of the victim and the assailant, as well as of the weapons used. You will also tell me just how long it took this little drama to unfold before your eyes from the beginning to end. Commence writing."

On the face of it, this should be an easy task, especially when we know that this is no ordinary class. All these students are graduate students majoring in psychology.

The results? One young man, who hopes to become a criminologist, writes: ". . . The killer was a big Germanic type. . . . Looked something like a Hollywood storm trooper. . . . Called the deceased an FBI man. . . . Said he was tired of being a Communist. . . . The murder weapon was a 7.5 Mauser. . . .The victim was a typical-looking student in his twenties . . . white . . . seasonable dress. . . ."

Another student, a young woman who hopes to become a clinical psychologist, says: ". . . The murderer was of average height . . . wearing a European-type railroad conductor's uniform. . . . Used a switch-blade knife on the victim. . . . Murderer said . . . 'You are a Marxist and are working to destroy our republic.'. . . Stabbed the victim three times . . . Victim was a white male dressed in khaki trousers and a blue sweater. . . ." And so on.

It was not mentioned by anyone that the "victim" of this assault was a black male, wearing an ROTC uniform!

The little episode just recounted gives something of an idea of the value of the eyewitness in court.

These students were highly trained in the art of observation. They had already spent at least four years studying human behavior, studying the many small nuances of the human mind. As "experts" they should be detached and should record events with precision.

If the experts can be wrong, what of the man in the street, who glimpses, for perhaps five seconds, another man running out of a liquor store, a bag marked money in one hand and a smoking pistol in the other? Or was it a pistol? Perhaps it was just a cigar.

In this age of noise, of gaudy motion, of incalculable distraction, it is impossible for the eye to record very much and even less possible for the memory to retain for long anything thus recorded.

But each day, in courtrooms all across the land, people take the stand and solemnly testify to events they would like us to believe they witnessed two years earlier.

Legal history abounds with cases of mistaken identity. Almost weekly we read of some person who, after spending ten or fifteen years in prison, is released because some eyewitness was mistaken. Innocent men have been executed because someone, under oath, testified that the accused was the same person who pulled a trigger or wielded a knife or was behind the wheel of a car.

Human memory is weak. Can you remember what you had for dinner three nights ago? What is your driver's license number? If you are a man and you have received military training, what was the serial number of your rifle? The serial number you were required to commit to memory? What is the color of your husband's—your wife's—eyes? In which hand does the Statue of Liberty carry a torch? Quickly, which direction is north? Finally, are you absolutely certain that you locked your front door last night before going to bed? Assuming that your life were at stake as a result of a false answer to *any* of the above questions, what would you say?

All of us would have to say: "I cannot be sure."

But what of the eyewitness in a criminal case? What of the people's witness who takes the stand and solemnly testifies that the accused, sitting a few feet away, was the person who held up his liquor store or who was seen running down a hotel corridor at three o'clock in the morning.

Our eyewitness had undoubtedly seen the accused, though perhaps not at the scene of the crime. The eyewitness' acquaintance with the accused probably commenced sometime after the crime had been committed. More likely than not, the victim and the accused were introduced through that age-old introduction bureau, the police department. To illustrate:

You are a small businessman. You own a combination liquor store and market. As a small businessman you probably have no other employees; you open the store in the morning and close it at night. In between, you arrange stock, wait on customers, beat off persistent salesmen, and try to get your bills paid on time. You are beset by most of the worries that confront all men: money; sickness;

taxes; dreams of a better tomorrow. Money comes in, and money goes out, and you hope that somewhere along the line enough of this money may stick to your fingers to allow you to retire.

It is late evening now. You have been on your feet for about ten hours. You are tired. You look at your watch, and like most people, you forget the time about five seconds later. You know, after looking at the watch, that you will be able to close up shop in a little while. Perhaps you light a cigarette or look at the day's receipts as you mark time, waiting to close. Your feet may hurt, for you have been standing for most of the day. In brief, your mind is probably distracted by a thousand-and-one little problems.

A man comes into the store. He walks to the refrigerator, opens it, takes out a six-pack of beer. Automatically, you know that this six-pack of beer retails for one dollar. If you see the man, you see him only as another customer, another face to smile at, another few pennies to add to your net profits for the day.

The man approaches, and perhaps he says, "And a package of cigarettes, too." You turn your back to get the cigarettes from a rack, and when you are facing the man again, he has a pistol pointed at your stomach.

"Give me the money," the man says.

What do you do? What do you think, standing less than two feet away from a man who, with pistol in hand, has just told you to give him ten hours of your hard labor? If you resist, he may shoot you. You have read, somewhere in yesterday's paper, that another little storeowner in this city was pistol-whipped and wounded by such a gunman. If you are able to think at all, while his pistol is trained on your stomach, you will probably think of your wife, your children, the unpaid insurance policy on your life, school for the youngest child, the operation your wife needs . . .

If you think at all, you will think that you do not want to die and better give him the money, the ten hours of your labor, than lie bleeding and dying on the floor as you pray that the ambulance will arrive in time to save your life.

You open the cash register, and you give the gunman the money. He stuffs it in his pocket and quickly leaves the store. In all, the whole transaction has taken less than ninety seconds.

You watch the man run down the dark street, see him get into a car. Then he is gone, and you are alone with your empty cash register. You are torn by emotion, for you saw death inside the muzzle of that man's pistol— and perhaps that was all you really saw as he stood before you, waiting for you to hand him the money.

You telephone the police, and you garble the message so that the police operator asks you to repeat it several times. Then you sit down, trembling, barely able to control yourself. You may be a little ashamed at how easily you were robbed. You may feel a great sense of relief that you were not pistol-whipped or shot.

But no matter how you feel, you do not feel normal.

You have been through a harrowing experience, something that has never happened to you before, and even as you wait for the police, you try to sort your thoughts, try to calm yourself, for you know that the police will have questions and you must have the answers.

The police arrive, and they *do* have questions. They want to know *your* name, *your* address. They want to know when the holdup took place. What was the exact time? What did the holdup man look like? Color of eyes? Color of hair? Color and style of clothing worn? Height? Weight? Peculiarities? Kind of gun? What did he say? How did he say it? Did he have a getaway car? Did he handle anything in the store?

Your mind is swimming as you try to make some sense out of these strange, new events. You want to tell the police: "This has never happened to me before; you must give me time to think." But the police are in a hurry. Perhaps one of the patrolmen gives you a few hints. Perhaps he says something that serves as a stimulus to your memory. Perhaps he shows you *his* gun and asks if it is similar to the gun the robber carried.

The police finally leave. You lock the store, trying to remember just what happened. Already, the whole thing seems to be a kind of hallucination. What *did* the holdup man look like? Somehow you have the impression that he looked something like your younger brother. Or maybe it was Robert Taylor, the movie star, whom he resembled. It is so hard to remember; so much happened, and the police asked so many questions.

But the police seemed to know what they were doing. This is their job, you tell yourself. They'll get the right man. They'd *better* get the right man; they're civil servants! You pay their wages.

When you get home, you tell your wife and your children about what happened to you. Neighbors come over. Everyone has questions to ask. Perhaps you add a little to the story, for now you may have the idea that you behaved badly in the store tonight. You didn't put up the kind of fight Humphrey Bogart would have fought had he been in your place. You didn't tell the stickup artist to go to hell. You didn't throw a bottle at him as he ran out of the store with your hard-earned money. You did none of these things, and although you have no right to feel ashamed, you still do.

Three days later the police telephone you. They believe they have the man who did it; just come down to the police station and identify him. Just a formality, they tell you; it is the same man.

You are a little relieved that the police have apprehended the man. Perhaps they recovered the money, too. As you hurry to the police station, any doubts you may have had about the holdup man's identity leave you. The police must know what they are doing. Sure! They have the right man. Just as on the television, they always get the right man. You smile and you feel a little proud of your police department. You'll have to remember to buy a ticket to the policemen's ball, next year.

Now you are inside the police station, in the lineup

room. The detective in charge of the case shows you a photograph of the suspect. He gives you plenty of time to study the features of the man in the photograph, both full face and profile. Yes, it *does* look like the man who held you up. You hand the photograph back to the detective, and he tells you that now some men will walk out on the stage in front of you. You will, in turn, tell him which of these men was the one who held you up.

Six men walk out onto the stage, their features lit up by the blinding white lights set in the ceiling. You scan the faces and you recognize one of these men; it is the same face you just looked at in the picture the detective handed you. No doubt about it!

"That's the man, Officer," you whisper, pointing at one of the men on the stage. "That's the man who held me up."

You leave the lineup room and sign a formal complaint. The police tell you that the suspect has a prior criminal record of some kind or other, while they may not tell you that the suspect was or was not found with the money from your store, with the pistol that was used in the robbery, or that he made a confession of guilt. They *have* told you he was an ex-convict, and that, to your way of thinking, is enough to satisfy you. Once a criminal, always a criminal.

A trial date is set, and you are in court. The district attorney puts you on the witness stand and asks you, in front of the twelve members of the jury, if you have ever seen the accused before.

"I have," you reply.

"When was the first time you saw the accused?"

You have memorized the date and the time of the robbery, as the district attorney before the trial suggested. You state, in a loud and firm voice, the date and time of the robbery. You go on to describe the events that took place perhaps three months ago. You have had time to think; you have seen the suspect in the lineup. The police never make mistakes on things like this, you tell yourself as the district attorney finishes his examination.

The accused is represented by a young man who only this year was admitted to the practice of law. He is a sincere and intelligent young man, but he lacks experience. He does not yet know how a lineup is conducted, how certain thoughts and conclusions may be put into a frightened witness' mind. The young lawyer does his best to rattle you, and that is the end of it.

The accused is found guilty. In accordance with the law, the accused is sentenced to prison for a period of not less than a certain number of years. As you leave the courtroom, you tell yourself he was lucky; any man who would pull a stickup ought to be sent up for life!

As the days pass, you forget much of what has happened to you. Perhaps you buy a pistol with the intention of using it on the next person who has the audacity to hold you up. You are regarded as something of a minor celebrity in the neighborhood for a while, and then even your neighbors forget about the holdup.

A year passes. One day you receive a letter from the man you helped send to jail. It is a short letter, asking you to search your soul, for he says he is innocent. The letter concludes with a plea to go to the police, tell them that you were mistaken in your identification. For a long moment you stare at the letter, then throw it in the wastebasket. A typical criminal trick, you tell yourself. There he is, stuck in prison for the next five years, trying to lie his way out.

You look at your watch—almost time to close. You go to the door of your shop, and just as you are about to throw the lock, the door opens and a man stands before you. He has a pistol in his hand, and it is pointed at your stomach.

It is the same man who held you up more than a year ago. It is not the same man you helped send to prison.

Trial by Jury

TRIAL by jury was secured to man as early as the Magna Carta, and our law has wisely placed the strong twofold barrier, of an indictment and a trial by jury, between the liberties of the people and the prerogative of the government.

The founders of our country contrived that no man should be called to answer for any capital crime unless upon the preparatory indictment by twelve or more of his fellow citizens—the grand jury—and that the truth of every accusation, whether by indictment or information, should afterward be confirmed by the unanimous verdict of twelve of his equals, indifferently chosen and above all suspicion.

However convenient new trial methods may appear at first, we realize that delays and little inconveniences in the forms of justice are the price that all free men must pay for their liberty.

The examination of witnesses in the presence of all

mankind is much more conducive to the clearing up of truth than the private and secret examination taken down in writing before an officer or his clerk, as was done in the ancient ecclesiastical courts, where a witness frequently deposed in private that which he would be ashamed to testify in a public trial.

An artful or careless reporter may make a witness speak what he never meant, by dressing up his deposition in his own form and language, but in open court the witness is at liberty to correct and explain his meaning, if misunderstood.

Besides, the occasional questions of the judge, the jury, and the counsel, propounded to the witnesses, will sift out the truth much better than a formal set of interrogatories previously written and settled, and the confronting of adverse witnesses is another opportunity of obtaining a clear discovery, which can never be had upon any other method of trial.

In short, the people who are to decide on the evidence have an opportunity of observing the quality, age, education, understanding, behavior, and inclinations of the witness.

When the evidence is gone through on both sides, the judge and the lawyers, in the presence of the parties, sum up the whole to the jury, observing wherein the main question and principal issue lies. The judge also gives the jury his opinion in the matter of law arising upon the evidence.

The jury, after the proofs are summed up, withdraws from the courtroom to consider its verdict till it is agreed on the verdict or is discharged because of its inability to do so.

A competent number of sensible and upright jurors, chosen by lot, will be found to be the best investigators of truth and the surest guardians of public justice, for the most powerful individual in the state will be cautious of committing any flagrant invasion of another's right when he knows that the fact must be examined and decided by twelve indifferent men and women, not appointed till the hour of trial, and that, when once the fact is ascertained, the law will redress it.

Every new tribunal, erected for the decision of facts, without the intervention of a jury is a step toward establishing the most oppressive of absolute governments. It is therefore on the whole a duty which every man owes to his country, his friends, his posterity, and himself, to maintain to the utmost of his power this valuable right and, above all, to guard with the most jealous circumspection against the introduction of new and arbitrary methods of trial, which, under a variety of plausible pretenses, may in time imperceptibly undermine this best preservative of liberty.

Sir William Blackstone in his *Commentaries on the Law of England* recommended that the best and most effectual method to preserve and extend the trial by jury in practice would be by endeavoring to remove all the defects, as well as to improve the advantages, incident to this mode of inquiry.

The principal defects seem to be: whether truthful and

71

unbiased answers are given by each juror while being examined under oath for jury duty to ascertain whether he can and will give a criminal defendant a fair and impartial trial and whether he will decide the case only upon the evidence introduced in court; or the possible danger to a defendant in a criminal case where the charge against him is of extensive local concern; or where the passions of the people have been enraged by the nature of the crime; or in a civil case where one of the parties is popular and the other is a stranger or obnoxious.

In all these cases, to summon a jury, laboring under local prejudices, is laying a snare for its consciences, and though they should have virtue and vigor of mind sufficient to keep them upright, the parties will grow suspicious.

Cross-Examination of the Jury

❦ ❦

MOST lawyers, judges, and jurors have not considered the impaneling of a jury as being part of the fine art of cross-examination, examining a large group of witnesses from which will be chosen the members of the trial jury.

This cross-examination delves into the juror's life: his thinking; his feeling toward the plaintiff or the defendant; his opinion of the law; his respect for the law; his understanding of the elements necessary to be proved to establish the cause of action or to convict for a crime.

Experienced trial lawyers study each juror carefully and learn by questions and answers his state of mind, as well as his ability to understand and to apply the law to the facts as presented by the evidence.

The good cross-examiner will weigh his every question. He will carefully walk the thorny path of educating the juror to his own theory of the case. He must be a good lawyer, as well as a shrewd judge of human nature.

The advantage of a jury is that there are twelve jurors.

The judgment of twelve persons instead of one brings more equitable results. Many trial lawyers can recall instances in which the judge, in reviewing the evidence in his charge to the jury, has misstated some of the evidence, even though he has taken notes.

A number of psychological studies made in recent years show that group decisions are fairer, more efficient, and more accurate in fact finding than are the decisions of an individual. The give-and-take of deliberation is the factor which makes the difference.

A dramatic example of the advantage of a jury over a judge is presented in *Quercia v. United States*. In that case, a federal district judge, commenting on the defendant's testimony, in his charge to the jury, said: "You may have noticed, Mr. Foreman and Gentlemen, that he wiped his hands during his testimony. It is rather a curious thing, but that is almost always an indication of lying. Why it should be we don't know, but that is the fact. I think that every single word that man said, except when he agreed with the Government's testimony, was a lie." The case was reversed by the Supreme Court.

If the district judge involved had been hearing a civil case without a jury, his half-baked and unsound psychological notions would have meant sure defeat for the unfortunate litigant who wiped his hands while testifying.

At a point lost in the mists of history there was woven into the philosophy of trial by the people the theory that law in its truest sense abides in the mind and heart of the people and that they collectively are its most just administrators.

Judges of our highest courts have contended that one of the purposes of the jury system is to permit the jury to temper strict rules of law by the demands and necessities of a substantial justice. The cross-examiner therefore must educate the jury to this principle.

Juries are composed of practical businessmen accustomed to thinking for themselves, experienced in the ways of life, capable of forming estimates and making nice distinctions, unmoved by the passions and prejudices to which court oratory is nearly always directed.

Of the greatest importance to the trial lawyer when he walks into court will be knowledge of the people who will constitute the jury. Jury lists are available to counsel, and he should avail himself of the list. He should study the names, and if necessary, look for these names in a city directory, learn where these people work, in what neighborhood they live. If he feels the need for greater investigation, he should call on an expert investigator for assistance. For when he starts cross-examining these prospective jurors on their acceptability to serve on the jury, he will have to know what to ask, to know when he is getting truthful answers. There is no shortcut to determine when a prospective juror is telling the truth. Only pretrial investigation of the juror's background will give the cross-examiner a basis for framing his questions.

Some trial lawyers who have chosen thousands of men and women to sit on civil and criminal juries have noted that what constitutes an acceptable juror is always a conclusion. But the advantage comes as a result of educating the panel to the facts and the law.

Some trial lawyers never select anyone with an obviously serious, somber, or sour disposition. Instead, they prefer smiles. This is an obvious conclusion and is frequently correct. The lawyer must take pains in his examination to determine that this dour juror is really what his expression indicates he is. Perhaps he is sad because the defendant is on trial for his life. Perhaps he is sour because his back has been injured in an automobile collision. Perhaps the case before him resembles one in which he was a party.

Other trial lawyers are wary of persons whose forebears were English, German, or Scandinavian. These persons tend to believe in absolute law enforcement and in severe punishment for anyone who runs afoul of the law. It is thought that such people are ultraconservative, bullheaded, and usually have their minds made up in advance of hearing testimony.

The outdoor or athletic type can take either side, and if convinced, he will espouse his cause with determination.

A Jew is acceptable only if the crime is a minor one; he is severe if the crime is one of violence. A brief examination of the history and of the cultural background of the Jew will explain his reasons for being severely opposed to violence. However, if the Jew is a man who is making his living as a bouncer in a saloon, it may be well to consider him as a favorable juror for the defense in an assault and battery case.

One hard-and-fast rule that has served well is: Never accept a wealthy person if the client is poor, nor a poor person if the client is wealthy. The gap between client and juror simply cannot be bridged.

A businessman is not the best juror if the client is a labor official, nor is the person who is in debt a good juror if the client is a banker or an official of a loan company.

A Southerner is often a good juror if the client is black, because the Southerner will often best understand the black's problems.

Actors and salesmen are almost always desirable; they have seen all sides of life and know the meaning of misfortune and suffering. By the same token, writers and artists also qualify as good jurors. And, of course, so do older men; the older man is more charitable and more understanding and forgiving than the young man.

In a criminal trial, minor officials, functionaries, religious zealots, super-Americans, and the like tend to take the words of the prosecutor as if they came from God. Such people have spent years in slavish obedience to authority, and naturally they have come to identify strongly with authority. To such men the very fact that the client is in court is enough. In their minds he is guilty.

Married men are more understanding and tolerant than bachelors. Women, of course, have always been—and always will be—a complete mystery.

Professional groups all over the country have made

77

exhaustive studies of jury personalities and have come up with their own results. A group from Fairleigh Dickinson University in New Jersey recently polled some five hundred persons of every imaginable background in a highly specific test designed to reveal the taint of prejudice, regardless of a person's race, creed, or color.

This poll concluded that there is a very small amount of pure-and-simple anti-black prejudice in today's juries. Generally speaking, the black juror tends to resent, slightly, the successful defendant, but the black man is more sympathetic toward youth, the out-of-work, and the poor. But a black banker would be a most dangerous juror if the defendant happened to be an indigent black man who was charged with robbing a pawnshop.

The five hundred who were tested showed little prejudice against the established religions such as Roman Catholicism, Judaism, or the many Protestant sects. There was prejudice felt toward some of the newer sects. As a result of those findings, perhaps it would be a good idea for the trial lawyer to advise his client to leave his copy of the *Watchtower* at home, should the defendant be on trial for a crime.

Certain occupational groups, according to the survey, cause the juror to bristle when he encountered them. Those toward whom the prospective juror is especially prejudiced are labor union officials and government functionaries. On the other hand, the study found that salesmen seem to be prejudiced against the unemployed, as well as people of Latin and Middle-European backgrounds. According to the studies, the salesman-juror tends to be favorably prejudiced toward the female defendant or plaintiff.

Oddly enough, a man stands a better chance of getting a fair trial from a jury than does a woman. According to the Fairleigh Dickinson poll, both men and women earning less than $5,000 a year are strongly prejudiced against women.

How much can a trial lawyer learn from a juror, based on what he says and how he presents himself? Not one of them will admit that he has carefully followed the case in the newspapers. On the contrary, when you ask if they have read the papers or watched television concerning your case, they will generally say no. But by probing them, you may develop that they have sneaked into the cellar and read the Scrutan ads by flashlight.

It has been said that the face is the mirror of the soul. This is not always true. Eichmann looked like a villain, but his chief, Himmler, looked like a man who could never form the intent to commit crime.

The cross-examiner must consider such factors as the juror's mode of dress. Is this man, for example, wearing what appears to be his only suit, and a threadbare one at that? He might be a good juror if the defendant is a poor man. He will be a bad juror if the client is a wealthy one.

Is this juror nervous and flighty? Does he wipe his lips frequently? Does he bite his fingernails? Does he pluck at his cuffs, or if the juror is a woman, does she pick at her nail polish? If so, here is a flighty mind at work—a mind that will be hard pressed to follow the case. And what about lodge rings, lapel decorations, and ornaments?

These are some of the signs that only courtroom experience can evaluate, but they are the small details that must not be ignored. If the client never saw military service and is charged with the crime of assault, the lawyer would do well to disqualify that juror who is frowning, whose name is MacPherson, and who wears a miniature Silver Star in his lapel buttonhole.

A jury trial is dramatic and complex, and the successful cross-examiner not only must keep his wits about him at all times, but must also know the rules. He must be keen and vital; he must understand something of men and their motives. He must remember that the litigants have reverted to their most primitive instincts and are now fighting like primordial animals, eager for victory, asking and giving no quarter.

From the moment the trial lawyer lays his papers on the counsel table his every act and word mean something to the jurors. Each will watch him. If he conducts himself properly, they will continue watching him and listening to his every word.

In his questions directed toward the prospective juror, the good cross-examiner will attempt to discover all he can about each juror, and he will often use what he has discovered to alert the juror to his, the lawyer's, theories about the case. The good trial lawyer will not make the mistake of thinking that one theory will suffice for all twelve jurors. It will not, no more than one line of reasoning will allow a parent to govern seven youngsters.

In the examination of the prospective juror, every question must mean something, either providing information for judging the juror or enabling the cross-examiner at this early stage of the trial to lay the foundation for his case.

A cross-examiner should never make it necessary for the juror to say he does not hear the question. If the juror is wearing a hearing aid or similar device, it is not necessary to shout at him. The lawyer should speak firmly and slowly, if necessary, but he should not make the juror feel either that he is unimportant or that the lawyer is obviously patronizing him. If the juror discerns that the lawyer is taking special care to be understood—without making a great show of such an elementary kindness—the juror will respect the lawyer for it.

In all cases, the cross-examiner should speak clearly and distinctly. Most laymen believe that the lawyer is a cultured and educated person. They are in court to see lawyers, and they have their own ideas of what a lawyer should be, how a lawyer should act. If a lawyer disappoints them, he is halfway toward losing them.

When we are about to meet someone important, we are always on our best behavior. This is how it should be when a lawyer first meets his prospective jury. He may never see any of these people again. Right now they are the most important people in his life; doubly important, for his client has entrusted his cause to him. When you have another's responsibilities to meet, they must always be more important than your own. This fundamentally is what being a good lawyer is all about.

The cross-examiner's questions should be framed as questions and not as assertions, even if he knows the answers in advance. Each question should be concise and certain and never argumentative. The questions must avoid assumptions and must in all cases call for direct answers.

Juries like to feel that their winning lawyer is made of the same stuff as they. Therefore, it is unwise for a lawyer to be too overtly brilliant. He should never by word or act permit the jury to feel that he thinks he is better than they.

A good cross-examiner should use simple and plain English when addressing a juror. He should not go off on semantic flights, nor should he go to the other extreme and keep his statements and questions on the level of a fourth-grade reading assignment.

The juror will have heard, somewhere along the line, that lawyers are a tricky body of skilled professionals who use legal terminology to cloud facts. The cross-examiner may counteract much of this propaganda by avoiding the usage of such words as "prior" and "subsequent," using instead "before" and "after."

The jury a lawyer first questions—and later addresses—has great responsibilities that weigh heavily upon its collective mind. It is all the jurors can do to sift through the mass of fact that confronts them. It is the lawyer's task to make them understand that fear, prejudice, malice, and the love of approbation bribe a thousand men, whereas gold bribes only one. But to the jury must go the credit for seeking and finding the truth.

Now some specifics: Bias of a juror may be actual or implied. Actual bias is the existence of a state of mind which leads to an inference that the person will not act with entire impartiality, while implied bias is that which is conclusively presumed to exist as a matter of law where the juror's interests and relationships have, by statute in many jurisdictions, been made the basis of disqualification of a juror. Where this is the case, proof need be made only of the existence of the interest or relationship; it is not necessary that bias or prejudice be shown to have in fact resulted therefrom.

Relationship within certain degrees of consanguinity or affinity is a ground for challenging a juror for cause. Even where such a rule is not applied or where the relationship is not within the prohibited degrees, it is important that questions be asked concerning such relationships since that fact, in conjunction with other answers elicited on *voir dire*, may tend to establish bias, prejudice, or hostility. Experience shows that men are prone to color their judgments, either consciously or unconsciously, so as to favor the interests of people related to them.

Where the relationship is not within the degrees of consanguinity or affinity which will permit challenge for cause, questions should be directed toward the degree of social relationship between the prospective juror and the party, his feelings toward the party, and whether, under the circumstances, he feels that he could render a fair and impartial verdict.

A juror who states that, by reason of his friendship with one of the parties to the action, he cannot be positive whether he could as readily render a verdict against such party as he could against a party not his friend is unquestionably biased in favor of his friend. Such bias may also stem from a friendship or acquaintance with one related to or closely associated with his friend.

Where there is a relationship or friendship between a prospective juror and the attorney for one of the parties, it may be fairly inferred that the prospective juror would be biased or partial toward the cause being represented by his relative or friend.

Bias or partiality may appear from a business or professional relationship existing or having existed between a prospective juror and the attorney for a litigant. This is especially true where favors or accommodations have been granted.

Probable bias or prejudice may be shown by the fact that a prospective juror is in the employ of a litigant or his attorney. This is true where he is dependent on the employment for his livelihood.

A juror will be disqualified on the ground of bias implied from an attorney-client relationship between him and an attorney for one of the parties where such relationship exists at the time of the trial. The prospective juror should, however, be questioned about a previous attorney-client relationship since this may develop evidence of actual bias or prejudice. For example, a prospective juror may have employed the attorney for one of the litigants in a case which he lost. He may feel that the attorney was responsible for the loss, and his hostility would prevent an impartial and unbiased judgment.

The fact that a prospective juror and a party or the attorney for a party are members of the same secret fraternal, social, religious, or political society or that the juror is a member of or contributor to an association for the suppression of certain types of crime does not of itself disqualify the juror in the absence of a showing that the association is connected with or in some manner interested in the particular case being tried. Questions about such memberships are permitted as an aid in exercising peremptory challenges or in discovering possible grounds of bias.

A bias arising from a juror's relationship to, friendship with, or acquaintance with a person known to be a prospective witness is a ground for challenge when the relationship is such that it would influence the weight the juror would give to the prospective witness' testimony.

The interest of a juror or his prior participation in the case being tried may, of itself, disqualify him, or it may be evidence of a disqualifying bias or prejudice. Generally, a juror is disqualified when it is shown that he is a party to, or is interested in, another civil suit or a criminal proceeding of the same character or involving the same controversy.

It is the duty of a juror during his *voir dire* examination to make full and truthful answers to questions. If he conceals or makes a false or misleading statement on any fact from which bias or interest may be inferred, this is misconduct which prejudices the rights of a litigant, for it impairs his right of challenge.

Generally, a juror in a personal injury action is not subject to challenge for cause because he previously had made claims or maintained suits for damages for personal injuries when none of the claims is shown to have been made against a party to the pending action. Questions on prior claims and litigation are very important even when they do not show sufficient bias or prejudice to sustain a challenge for cause. They may give the party making the inquiry sufficient suspicion of prejudice to exercise a peremptory challenge.

A juror who has formed an opinion on a material issue or fact in the case, which will require strong and positive evidence to overcome, is not unbiased. The questioning need show only that the juror has formed an opinion; it is not necessary that he shall have expressed or declared such an opinion before being called as a juror.

A juror is not incompetent to serve because he has formed an opinion about the case and says it will take evidence to change this opinion, but states that he can fairly and impartially try the case according to the law and the evidence and render a true verdict.

Disqualified is the juror who says that it would require strong and positive evidence to overcome the opinion, or expresses a doubt about whether he could lay the opinion aside, or states that he would not be willing, if he were the challenging party, to have his case tried by a juror in his frame of mind.

Bias may arise from the interest a juror has as a stockholder, officer, director, or employee of a corporation that is a party to the action or from his relationship to one who is so interested. In the latter case, it must be shown that the juror knows of the interest of the related person.

The trial lawyer may question prospective jurors on *voir dire* respecting their interest in or connection with liability insurance companies. Connection with or interest in a liability insurance company that has issued a policy of insurance protecting the litigant against liability for negligence is a fact from which bias may be inferred.

Experience has shown that jurors are more likely to find that liability exists and to return verdicts larger in amount when they are informed that the defendant has insurance protection than otherwise.

In some jurisdictions the right to question jurors about their interest in or connection with liability insurance companies does not exist absolutely, but depends on a preliminary showing, usually required to be made in the absence of the jury or by affidavit, that the counsel believes, or is informed, or knows that the defendant is insured, that the insurance company is participating or is interested in the outcome of the case, and that counsel knows, or has reasonable cause for belief, that one or more of the prospective jurors has a disqualifying interest.

The scope and extent of the questioning and the form

which questions must take vary greatly. Some jurisdictions confine the inquiry to the interest of jurors in "any" insurance company furnishing protection against liability for negligence. Others permit questioning on a particular insurance company, but the questions must be so phrased that the matter of the defendant's insurance protection is not needlessly stressed.

Generally, the existence of racial prejudice which may affect a juror's attitude toward the parties or issues is a proper ground for inquiry, but there is great difference of opinion on the extent to which such examination may be carried or the questions that may be asked.

Some courts consider that a general question of whether the juror can, under all circumstances, give the parties a fair and impartial trial, in accordance with the law and the evidence, is sufficiently broad and comprehensive to embrace any question of prejudice, and if answered affirmatively, there is no need for specific questions on racial prejudice.

There is a natural tendency for people, when questioned directly, to deny that they hold any prejudices against a particular race or nationality. Many attorneys have found it the better practice to so word their questions as to obtain from the juror an affirmative promise that he will not allow any prejudice he might have to influence his verdict. In this field, inquiries into a juror's religious beliefs are generally excluded unless there are religious issues involved or special circumstances which would raise the possibility of religious prejudice.

Where a juror has a fixed and abiding bias or prejudice against certain types of actions which he has entertained for some time, which he has frequently expressed, and to which he still adheres, he is disqualified with respect to an action falling in such a class.

Many people hold prejudices regarding such defenses as insanity or self-defense. Often the prejudice results from a lack of understanding of the principles on which such defenses are based. Questioning on *voir dire*, therefore, is not only a means of discovering bias or prejudice, but an opportunity for counsel to explain the reasoning on which a particular defense is founded and thus to create a more receptive mood for the evidence he will offer on that issue.

A juror who has such a strong prejudice against taking cases on contingent fees that he believes any attorney who takes a case on that basis should not receive anything is disqualified.

Questioning each juror in detail is likely to be, to the juror, a tiresome and boring process, and such a tactic is likely to create an unfavorable impression. To avoid this, use can be made of general questions after the first two or three jurors have been examined in detail, only the more important questions being asked of subsequent jurors.

Generally, a court is not bound by the answers of a juror on his *voir dire* examination, but may consider other evidence in determining his competency, and when the juror states that he has formed an opinion about the case, courts will permit a full investigation of such an opinion.

Extrinsic testimony or that elicited by cross-examination to show the bias or interest of a juror covers a wide range and the field of external circumstances from which probable bias or interest may be inferred is infinite, encompassing all facts and circumstances which, when tested by human experience, tend to show that the juror may color his thinking for the purpose of helping to establish one side of a cause.

To Watch or Not to Watch

No man has the choice of his mental or physical makeup or of where, when, and how he was born. Measuring a man by his physical appearance does not always aid in ascertaining the truth of testimony on the witness stand.

Some experienced cross-examiners think it is necessary to watch the witness constantly in an attempt to learn what he is thinking by the manner in which he reacts to questions on both direct and cross. Often questions on direct examination cause the witness to change his expression, to hesitate in answering, or to change the tone of his voice. The uncertain witness asks to have questions repeated time and again to give him time to frame his answers.

There are times, of course, when watching the witness does not pay off. I have yet to see a confidence man who did not look me straight in the eye. This is the swindler's first accomplishment; his second is an air of overwhelming frankness. Therefore, the exception often proves the

91

rule, and application and trial experience will let you pick between the liar and the honest but mistaken witness.

There is a continuing debate among experts on what to consider in evaluating the witness. Some exclude the feature of muscular development. Some contend the structure of the nervous system may be modified by learning or training, aside from effects of heredity. Others assume that there is a linkage between states of nervous mechanism and mental traits, but these neural conditions are not directly observable.

The best rule may be for each trial lawyer to make his own rules based on his experience. As we have said, great care should be used not to fall into the error of the judge who told a jury that when the defendant wiped his hands during his testimony, it was an indication that he was lying. The judge did not realize that increased activity of the sweat glands accompanies emotional stress. Sweating by a witness may be due to the heat in the courtroom, the stress of the unusual act of testifying, the strain of the facts to him personally, or his dread of cross-examination. All these are consistent with his telling the truth.

Judge Leo R. Friedman, one of the country's distinguished trial lawyers, noticed that a district attorney did not ask a key prosecuting witness where he lived. Judge Friedman asked the question on cross-examination, and since the witness was evasive, Friedman kept pressing, asking his address time and again without getting a satisfactory answer. The witness was shifty, and when it was finally brought out that he lived in the county jail, it was apparent to all that he was not only a jailbird, but evasive besides, and the value of his evidence was practically nil.

The trial lawyer who takes detailed notes of the witness' testimony is missing the opportunity to observe and determine the best way to handle the witness. A few brief notes may be justified, but the examiner's attention should be concentrated on the total recall of the vital facts.

Careful attention should be given to details. It is well to concentrate on the main events, but do not disregard seemingly unimportant bits of evidence. Often insignificant facts unravel the skein of evidence. If a man understands the significance of the unimportant things, no one can lie to him.

A shifty eye usually means nothing but shyness; a restless manner is simply a restless manner; hesitation indicates as often as not an effort to be accurate.

The liars are spotted by judges and juries by self-contradiction and inconsistency—not by their voices or appearances. Appearances are many times deceitful. We meet a man with the appearance and bearing of a General of the Army, and he proves to be untruthful and irresponsible.

Many have tried to analyze character, temperament, and abilities by the dimensions of the forehead, prominence of the chin, shape of the nose, convexity of the profile, texture of the skin and hair, and other morpho-

93

logical aspects governed by metabolism and skeletal growth rather than by behavior.

There is little to justify the claims of character analysts that their methods constitute an exact science. Behavior and evidences of behavior seen in the face are sometimes reliable evidence of the mental makeup of a witness, but from a scientific point of view it may be accepted that the anatomical features of the individual are determined by heredity. It does not take the brain of a genius to explain that training has no effect on the shape and size of the nose, the shape of the ears, the form of the mouth, the color and texture of the hair, or any other structural feature. The size of the head and its shape or the size or the color of the eyes have no relation to mentality.

You as the cross-examiner must consider the demeanor and the behavior of the witness on the witness stand: the witness' manner of testifying; whether the witness impresses you as a truthful individual; whether the witness impresses you as having an accurate memory and recollection; whether the witness has any motive for not telling the truth; whether the witness had full opportunity to observe the matters concerning which he has testified; whether the witness has any interest in the outcome of the case or friendship or animosity toward other people concerned in the case.

You must consider the reasonableness or unreasonableness, the probability or improbability, of the testimony in determining whether to accept it as true and

94

accurate, whether the witness has been contradicted or corroborated by other credible evidence.

If the witness has shown himself to be biased or prejudiced against you, it must be determined whether such bias or prejudice has colored his testimony so as to affect his desire and capability to tell the truth.

More can be learned from the poise and attitude of the witness. The real emotional process becomes manifest when faced with definite conditions. The play of the emotions of the witness often aids in interpreting his aim and purpose. Whether he is answering truthfully or not soon becomes apparent to a close observer. Fear, hope, anger, hate, grief, surprise, and love are difficult to disguise.

To watch or not to watch the witness becomes part of the experience of the trial lawyer. Each cross-examiner must find the way easiest and most profitable for him.

Dangers of Cross-Examination

JOHN HENRY WIGMORE, greatest of the exponents of the law of evidence, has said:

> Not even the abuses, the mishandlings, and the puerilities which are so often associated with cross-examination have availed to nullify its value. It may be that in more than one sense it takes the place in our system which torture occupied in the medieval system of the civilians. Nevertheless, it is beyond any doubt the greatest legal engine ever invented for the discovery of truth.
>
> However difficult it may be for the layman, the scientist, or the foreign jurist to appreciate its wonderful power, there has probably never been a moment's doubt upon this point in the mind of a lawyer of experience. . . . He may, it is true, do more than he ought to do; he may make the worse appear the better reason to perplex and —maturest counsels—may make the truth appear like falsehood. But this abuse of its power is able to be remedied by proper control.
>
> The fact of this unique and irresistible power remains, and is the reason for our faith in its merits. If we omit political considerations of broader range, then cross-

examination, not trial by jury, is the great and permanent contribution of the Anglo-American system of law to improved methods of trial procedure.

Cross-examination is a necessary art used to trap the unwilling or dishonest witness, but its use is dangerous for the trial lawyer. It may fail to make a witness remember what he has forgotten and sometimes will make him testify falsely.

Error in testimony is the rule rather than the exception. Pressing a witness with questions days, weeks, or months after the event may cause him to believe that he observed or remembers something that he did not see or does not remember.

It is not the voluntary errors in testimony which are most dangerous; rather, it is the involuntary ones. But the greatest danger confronting the trial lawyer is the effect of mistaken evidence.

Words are a vital issue in a trial. When the witness is asked to remember a story, his reproduction consists almost entirely of paraphrase. Accuracy of reproduction, in a literal sense, is the rare exception and not the rule. A witness generally does not testify in the precise words used, but his understanding of the purport of what was said may not coincide with what was expressed. The degree to which circumstances corroborate one another and the intrinsic probability of the matter sworn to are a far better test of truth than any oath can possibly be.

Great stress is laid on the advantage enjoyed by the

judge and jury, who are able to study the witness while he is being examined. This is one reason for the open court proceeding, the theory being that the detection of falsehood or uncertainty is facilitated by seeing and hearing the witness give evidence. However, it is an exaggeration to suppose that a lie can be detected merely by observing the way in which the witness utters it, for some liars are bold and some honest witnesses are hesitant and nervous. All who have experience in trying cases can testify to this, though the jury may be unaware of it.

Those who are always in the courts have learned that it is by no means always the shrewd and fully confident witness who is speaking the truth. On the contrary, those who have reluctantly come to court and who are very nervous by being there at all are apt to give their evidence in a hesitating manner and, indeed, often to contradict themselves and forget things which they remembered before they got on the witness stand. The confidence with which a witness recalls an event is no guide to the accuracy of his recollection.

There is a sharp distinction between fact and opinion. The ordinary witness is supposed to speak only of what he actually knows, as opposed to deduction or inference, which is a matter of opinion to be decided by the jury. No firm line can be drawn in recollection between observation and inference.

When the story to be remembered contains some puzzling elements, witnesses show a strong tendency to rationalize, which means that they will tell the story as they think it ought to have been rather than as it was. Whenever anything appeared incomprehensible, it was either omitted or explained.

Errors of observation and recall are helped by conditions such as darkness, momentary fleeting observation, emotion, suggestion, and lapse of time since the occurrence.

Suggestion often takes the form of autosuggestion, where the witness brings himself to believe something in which he wishes to believe or where he succumbs to the influence of another.

The most striking example of suggestion is group suggestion, when some strong collective emotion operates to distort what is perceived and remembered. Although it now rarely affects legal proceedings, superstitious suggestion is by no means extinct in modern times.

The questioning of a witness, though it adds details to his testimony, also increases the risk of error. Such questioning, whether before or at the trial, is necessary to direct the witness' mind to the points that need to be established, as well as to overcome a possible reluctance to speak or to detect falsification, yet it necessarily affects the truth of the answers.

The form of the question may call up a representation associated with it, particularly one that has been most often joined with it, or the question may reveal to the witness a gap in his recollection, which he seeks to fill by trying different possibilities by outright lying.

The law forbids counsel to ask his own witness lead-

99

ing questions at the trial. He may ask leading questions on cross-examination, which may trap a lying witness into revealing the truth. Even if the witness is honest, his confidence in what he is saying can be shaken.

It is impossible in a court of law to place confidence in the evidence of a witness who can be reduced in cross-examination to saying, "I do not remember," even though there is the possibility that his first statement was right.

People often make statements to the police under a strong sense of public obligation, but they do not generally regret escaping the embarrassments of public appearance for examination and cross-examination on the witness stand. They are not generally anxious to be publicly associated with an unsavory case. They tend to believe that if the police do not call them as witnesses, they are unnecessary witnesses. When they are approached by the defense, they are inclined to be resentful or suspicious or to think they are being dragged in without need. They can, of course, be compelled by subpoena to come to court and give evidence. But few lawyers would take the risk of calling a witness without knowing what evidence he is likely to give.

Memory generally fades with the passage of time, and when a witness is required to recall an event more than once, his act of recall on a subsequent occasion may be merely an imperfect memory of what he said earlier.

The danger to an accused arises when the witness, through a trick of memory, believes that he saw or heard what he did not.

Tests for Credibility

BEFORE cross-examining, the trial lawyer will evaluate the credibility of the witness. Consideration must be given to any matter that has a tendency in reason to prove or disprove the truthfulness of his testimony, such as:

(1) His demeanor while testifying and the manner in which he testifies;

(2) The character of his testimony;

(3) The extent of his capacity to perceive, to recollect, or to communicate any matter about which he testifies;

(4) The extent of his opportunity to perceive any matter about which he testifies;

(5) His character for honesty or veracity or their opposites;

(6) The existence or nonexistence of a bias, interest, or other motive;

(7) A statement previously made by him that is consistent with his testimony;

(8) A statement made by him that is inconsistent with any part of his testimony;

(9) The existence or nonexistence of any fact testified to by him;

(10) His attitude toward the action in which he testifies or toward the giving of testimony;

(11) His admission of untruthfulness;

(12) His prior conviction of a felony.

Probabilities

In litigation the trial lawyer must find the probable truth, and in forming his opinion of the truth of facts, he must exercise an active imagination and a knowledge of life and of men and should be guided by the greater number of probabilities on the one side as against the other. Absolute certainty is seldom attained in human affairs.

In addition to experience, it is hard work and preparation for the trial which will enable him to handle the circumstances which at first appear disconnected and valueless but which may, if skillfully handled, become united and ensure conviction in the mind of the judge or the jury.

If the trial lawyer has thought intently on the subject which he seeks to develop in court and has sought for signposts to follow to the true solution of the litigation, he will see facts which the less thoughtful would pass by. Careful study of the case before it comes to trial will

103

usually open routes for successful cross-examination to the probabilities of a story.

The majority of cases are composed of a few main facts enclosed in a circle of minor ones. No trial lawyer should depend solely on direct testimony about the main facts, but on the supporting probabilities brought to light by developing evidence of minor facts.

Acts and conversations inconsistent with human knowledge and experience are properly rated as improbable. Men will accept as probable that which they would have done or said under similar conditions.

Probability is an element which addresses itself to the reason and is frequently invoked in matters of human conduct and experience for determining the existence or nonexistence of a fact. The jury may determine an issue of fact as its probability or improbability may appear from the evidence.

If any proposition in the case appears to be probable, it is likely to be true. When a proposition is probable, it is supported by evidence which inclines the mind to believe, but leaves some room for doubt.

In searching for probability in evidence, we must consider probative facts which address themselves to reason and give grounds for belief. Probability is susceptible of being taken as meaning reasonable, and in turn, "reasonable" is synonymous with "probable."

The search for probabilities is a hazardous occupation for the inexperienced. There is great danger of bringing out some incidental circumstance that serves only to confirm or corroborate the statements of a witness made before the cross-examination began. In this search it is well to remember that accidental testimony always makes a great impression on a juror's mind. Beware!

Identification Evidence

It is inevitable that some miscarriages of justice should take place under any system of law, and the best that can be hoped and worked for is that these mishaps should be kept to a minimum.

The major source of error is the identification of the accused by the victim of a crime of violence. This mistake is alone responsible for many convictions, and pathetically, the wrongfully accused person and the guilty criminal usually bear not the slightest resemblance to each other.

Faces seem peculiarly liable to set up attitudes and consequent reactions which are largely colored by feeling. They are rarely analyzed in much detail. We rely on a general impression, obtained at the first glance.

Error of recognition breeds an invincible assurance in the witness, highly deceptive for those who are not forewarned of the possibility. There is no difference, from the subjective point of view, between true and false recognition, so far as their intrinsic qualities are concerned, and there are no objective signs to distinguish one from the other. The witness' certainty may not be immediate without this delay's being necessarily a sign of error.

Resemblance is a matter of relativity. For a white person, all blacks are like one another, and conversely. A person can much better distinguish those of his own age and condition than those of different ages and conditions.

Juries do not recognize the unreliable nature inherent in identification evidence by comparative strangers to the accused, and the good trial lawyer will prepare the jury for such dangerous visually imperfect evidence.

Granting a reasonably good memory on the part of the witness, the danger of the showup is that the witness expects to find the guilty person present and therefore points out the man who he thinks is most like the one he remembers. Thus, all that a showup can really be said to establish is that the accused resembled the criminal more closely than any other members in the showup did.

Invented Evidence

LOYALTY or a desire for revenge will pervert a witness' evidence. Some types of evidence have been found by experience to be so liable to false invention that, though they remain admissible, special safeguards have been devised for them.

The prosecution may have a confession from one of a gang, who is ready to turn state's evidence against his companions. This evidence must be scrutinized with care, because the informant is anxious to stand well with the police in order to protect himself from prosecution or to reduce his own sentence.

When several accused people are charged jointly and one of them gives evidence on his own behalf, he may be cross-examined with a view to implicating his companions. This course may be taken even though the only evidence given in chief by him is that he is guilty. Any admissions he makes in direct or cross-examination become evidence in the case as a whole and are therefore evidence against the co-defendants. The co-defendants are entitled to cross-examine the defendant giving the evidence.

Where the evidence of an accomplice becomes admissible against his co-defendants, it remains suspect evidence because of its tainted source. The accomplice may no longer have anything to fear or hope from the way in which he gives his evidence, yet he may entertain such a fear or hope, or he may wish by his evidence against others to gratify some spite against them; the circumstances make it easy for him because as a confederate he knows the inner story of what has happened, thus implicating in it one who is perhaps innocent.

Justice and fair dealing provide the law which prohibits convicting a defendant on the uncorroborated evidence of an accomplice. It is the law that judges must warn juries of the need for corroboration.

The Burden of Proof

EVERY man is presumed to be innocent until he is proved guilty to a moral certainty and beyond reasonable doubt.

When a man has been indicted by a grand jury or has been held to answer by a committing magistrate, it has already been officially determined that there is a prima facie case against him. Obviously such a man is not, in any intelligible sense outside the rules of the law of evidence, presumed to be innocent, though neither is he presumed to be guilty.

The fact simply is that the finger of suspicion is pointing against him. We must, however, do everything possible to treat such a man as if he were innocent, consistent with the demands of the public safety and the due trial of the charge. Generally our treatment of defendants after arrest and before trial is a repudiation of the philosophy behind the supposed presumption of innocence.

When it is said that a defendant is presumed to be in-

110

nocent, what is really meant is that the burden of proving his guilt is on the prosecution.

But there are situations, such as the shifting burden under Section 5851 of the Internal Revenue Code:

> It shall be unlawful for any person to receive or possess any firearm which has at any time been transferred in violation of sections. . . . Whenever on trial for a violation of this section the defendant is shown to have or to have had possession of such firearm, such possession shall be deemed sufficient evidence to authorize conviction, unless the defendant explains such possession to the satisfaction of the jury.

If it is impossible for the prosecution to give wholly convincing evidence on certain issues from its own hand, it is therefore up to the accused to give evidence on them if he wishes to escape.

Judges must direct juries that a crime has to be proved beyond reasonable doubt. This requires a clear conviction of guilt and not merely a suspicion, even a strong suspicion, though on the other hand a mere fanciful doubt where it was not in the least likely to be true would not prevent conviction.

I Object

DURING a trial, lawyers and judges are in eternal war to determine whether evidence is or is not irrelevant, immaterial, or incompetent. There is no precise test of relevancy; the question must be determined in each case according to reason and judicial experience. Materiality is much the same as relevancy, and incompetency covers a multitude of sins.

It is fairly common practice to use the terms "relevant" and "material" and particularly their opposites—"irrelevant" and "immaterial"—as interchangeable and synonymous. Although "relevant" is the broader term and is often used in the double sense of relevant and material, the distinction between the two concepts is substantial.

A "material matter" is one the existence or nonexistence of which is provable in the action. Materiality depends on the issues in the case; evidence which does not relate to a matter in issue is immaterial.

No proposition can be evidenced except that which is properly in issue under the substantive law and the pleadings. A fact evidencing a proposition not properly in issue is inadmissible, because immaterial, commonly called collateral.

Evidence that is within the issues, and therefore material, but is of slight probative value or significance in the case, has been described as immaterial. To eliminate this confusing loose usage, the Evidence Code substitutes the word "disputed" for "material" and covers this correct concept of materiality in the single definition of "relevant evidence." "Remoteness" thus becomes a ground of discretionary exclusion.

The law of evidence requires that evidence to a jury shall be relevant, and not slightly so; it must not afford a basis for conjecture, but for real belief; it must not be remotely relevant, but proximately so.

Again, it must not unnecessarily complicate the case or tend to confuse, mislead, or tire the minds of the jury or to withdraw their attention from the real issues of the case. In the application of such standards as these, the chief appeal is made to sound judgment and the discretion of the judge.

Relevancy is concerned with the probative quality of the evidence offered. Relevancy, as the word itself indicates, is not an inherent characteristic of any item of evidence but exists as a relation between an item of evidence and a proposition sought to be proved. Relevancy is the tendency of the evidence to establish a material proposition. Evidence is relevant not only when it tends to prove or disprove the precise fact in issue, but when it tends to establish a fact from which the existence or

113

nonexistence of the fact in issue can be directly inferred.

The Model Code of Evidence includes materiality in the concept of relevancy, but uses the term "disputed" instead of "material." The Evidence Code definition is: "Relevant evidence means evidence, including evidence relevant to the credibility of a witness or hearsay declarant, having any tendency in reason to prove or disprove any disputed fact that is of consequence to the termination of the action."

The test of materiality must be applied to any kind of evidence. But the concept of relevancy is normally discussed in connection with circumstantial evidence and not testimonial evidence. The reason is that in the case of testimony the only inference sought to be drawn is the truth of the fact from the witness' statement of it. Hence, questions of relevancy arise only in respect to circumstantial evidence, both documentary or real.

In handling the vast multitude of cases in which courts and writers have attempted impossible distinctions between logically relevant and legally relevant evidence, the Model Code of Evidence gets back to first principles. It defines relevant evidence as evidence having any probative value upon any matter the existence or nonexistence of which is provable in the action. It then makes all relevant evidence admissible except as otherwise specifically provided and entrusts to the trial judge the power to exclude relevant evidence the probative value of which is outweighed by the risks which its reception would carry.

One of the functions of pleadings is to limit the issues and narrow the proofs. If facts alleged in the complaint are not controverted by the answer, they are not in issue, and no evidence need be offered to prove their existence. Evidence which is not pertinent to the issues raised by the pleadings is immaterial.

It follows, therefore, if an issue has been removed from a case by an admission in the answer, no evidence which is material solely to the excluded matter may be received. This does not mean, for example, that an admission of liability precludes a plaintiff from showing how an accident happened if such evidence is material to the issue of damages. In an action for personal injuries, where liability is admitted and the only issue to be tried is the amount of damage, the force of the impact and the surrounding circumstances may be relevant and material to indicate the extent of plaintiff's injuries.

While the trial judge may, in his discretion, exclude cumulative, although relevant, evidence to avoid confusing the jury or wasting the time of the court, a different rule applies to evidence offered with respect to an issue entirely removed by the pleadings. Such evidence is not merely cumulative on a material issue, but is completely irrelevant, and there is no room for the exercise of discretion.

Trial judges are often told by cross-examiners, when the objection "not proper cross-examination" is made, that their questions are merely testing the veracity, interest, or bias of the witness. Too often, however, the cross-examiner is proceeding along the lines that do not test for veracity or other elements of credibility. If the judge stops him, he often insists that any question may be asked of the witness so long as his (the examiner's) sole object is to test for credibility. But unless the questions asked are properly framed so as to test the veracity, interest, or bias of the witness or are limited to a cross-examination of material facts brought out on the direct examination, the questions are improper.

The cross-examiner, over apt objection, is not entitled under the guise of "testing" to expand his right of cross-examination to develop material facts not testified to by the witness on the direct examination. Whether an objection is made or not, the trial judge is under a duty to restrict the cross-examiner who piles up a record to no purpose.

Cross-examination is limited to delving into the material facts brought out on direct examination, but the cross-examiner may test the veracity, interest, or bias of the witness by such questions only as directly test the veracity, interest, or bias of the witness or other elements going to his credibility, such as if he has been convicted of a felony.

There is no basis for the belief that "time, place, and persons present" are a required "foundation" for the proof of any conversation.

It is not necessary to fix time, place, and circumstances of alleged statements made by a defendant by questioning him thereon before proving such statements. His declarations and statements are original evidence.

I Object

Objections are made to the relation of conversations on the ground of "no foundation laid." There is no such objection. Only where the subject matter of the conversation is used for the purpose of impeachment is it necessary to lay a foundation of time, place, and persons present. If opposing counsel deems the circumstances of time, place, and persons present to be important, he is free to bring them out in cross-examination.

It is true that before one can impeach a witness by separate proof of a prior inconsistent statement, a proper foundation, including time, place, and persons present, must be laid. But cross-examination on a conversation does not require such foundation, which is a condition precedent only to separate proof of an allegedly impeaching statement. The objection of lack of foundation is proper when the impeaching witness is on the stand, not during cross-examination of the witness to be impeached.

Grounds for objection are:

Incompetent
Irrelevant
Immaterial
Leading and suggestive
Calling for a conclusion
Asked and answered
Argumentative
Assuming facts not
    in evidence
Not the best evidence
Hearsay
Beyond the scope

Compound question
Complex question
Unintelligible
Opinion by nonexpert
No proper foundation
Self-incrimination
No corpus delicti
Privileged communication
Cumulative
Self-serving
Improper impeachment
    of own witness

Take Five

IN recent years the Fifth Amendment words "nor shall be compelled in any criminal case to be a witness against himself" have been the subject of interminable debate.

While they may have protected some criminals, they have also protected the innocent from hate or revenge.

The cross-examiner knows that if the witness answers truly, he will be convicted for a violation of law; if he answers falsely, he will be convicted of perjury; if he refuses to answer, he will be found guilty of criminal contempt and punished by fine and imprisonment.

This Fifth Amendment clause has a long history. In the sixteenth century it was brought forward in England in protest against the inquisitorial method of the ecclesiastical courts. During this time the common law permitted accused defendants to be questioned. After 1660 it became a fixed rule that no one was compelled in any criminal case to be a witness against himself.

It is not generally known, but a witness in a civil proceeding may also refuse to answer any question his answer to which might be used against him in any criminal proceeding.

The right of a witness to refuse to give evidence that may tend to incriminate him is applicable in state as well as in federal courts because the Fourteenth Amendment requires the states to enforce this Fifth Amendment right.

Only the witness who is being examined may claim the right personally or through his lawyer.

The cross-examiner is concerned whether the witness has protected his rights. If the witness has preserved these federal rights and has claimed expressly the protection against self-incrimination granted by the Fifth and Fourteenth Amendments to the Constitution, the cross-examination must end.

The Fifth Amendment protection also excludes from evidence in a criminal case a defendant's statements made during in-custody interrogation without first being adequately warned of his constitutional rights. The protection does not apply to evidence that is not of a testimonial or communicative nature, such as fingerprints, handwriting exemplars, or specimen body fluids.

No presumption arises against the witness who avails himself of this right. The judge or jury must not draw any inference from it, nor may the cross-examiner comment on it.

If the question asked the witness on cross-examination pertains directly to offenses for which prosecution is barred, he must answer. But if the question relates to a misdemeanor, which is outlawed in one year, and the answer may expose the witness to prosecution for *conspiracy* to commit the misdemeanor (a felony), for which the statutory period is three years, he need not answer.

If a statute or constitutional provision grants a witness immunity from prosecution for any offense of which the compelled evidence might tend to prove him guilty, he must testify.

To grant immunity, an order of the court is required. The prosecution cannot make this request until the witness has claimed the right, and the judge must give the witness an opportunity to oppose the request.

A witness who claims the right against self-incrimination must prove that the proffered evidence might tend to incriminate him. He may point out the implications of the question, the setting in which it is asked, circumstances subjecting him to suspicion of crime, or other circumstances affecting the likelihood of his being criminally punished as a result of his answer. Here the cross-examiner will tread not only softly, but firmly.

Your Own Witness

CROSS-EXAMINATION can be the curse of a lawyer's life. So can the interrogation of your own client bring disaster, the pitfall being the same—asking that one question too many.

A landlord wanted his tenant, an attractive young widow with a child, evicted on the grounds that her conduct was questionable. He complained that she made too much noise and had too many visitors at all hours of the day and night.

In this case, cross-examination proved to be beneficial. The landlord admitted grudgingly that he had made similar accusations that had been proved unfounded against previous tenants.

The mood of the jurors indicated to courtroom observers that the case would be decided in favor of the attractive widow. There was no need to put her on the stand, but her lawyer did just that:

Q. What is your name?

A. Mary Jones.

Q. What did you say to Mr. Flowers in connection with renting the apartment?

A. I told him I was a widow who needed a home for me and my little boy.

Q. What is your son's name?

A. James Smith.

Q. Oh, is he your son by another husband?

A. No, by a friend.

Exemplars

THE art of cross-examination with all the pitfalls, heart-breaks, and anxieties is nevertheless the most potent weapon when carefully used.

In our adversary system in criminal trials and in civil differences, we see a creaking monster preying on the misfortunes and tribulations of man, where one question may change his future, may send him to the penitentiary, may deprive him of his assets, may belittle him, and may cost him his life.

It is inevitable that there are many trial lawyers who, without preparation and study of their cases, will dash in without the realization of their responsibility to weigh carefully every question and to anticipate every answer.

In the trial of cases the cross-examiner must realize that he is on a road without directional signs. He must lay his course by a star which he has never seen.

The following pages of actual cross-examination give some idea of the form that may be used. But every trial lawyer has his own style, his own thoughts, and his own purposes. The examples which follow are perhaps of more value as entertainment than as guides for cross-examiners.

The People v. Wong

❧⸙❧

AT 4 A.M. the police arrived. Inspector Gariott found Tom Yick dead in a pool of blood outside the closed door of Wong's apartment. Three bullets had hit him. Mrs. Wong, fully dressed when she answered the inspector's knock, said she had heard some shots but that her husband usually handled such things.

Inspector Gariott found Wong reading some applications for a bookkeeping job. The 38-caliber pistol which he readily admitted having fired at Yick lay on his desk. Wong carefully squared his conservative businessman's hat and walked with the officers to the Hall of Justice, where he calmly dictated a statement to the police stenographer: "I went home and I was talking to my wife at nighttime. I heard a knock at the door. Then I opened it. I saw it was Tom Yick, and I thought he was going to do something to me. I pulled the gun out to knock his head with the gun, and the bullet came out then. It went through his head. Then I left."

Despite their endless noisy chatter, the Chinese became taciturn as turtles in the face of Occidental justice.

125

The wife avoided intimate details of her relationship with Yick. Wong himself, after his first confession, became thoughtfully silent. Not a shadow crossed his face when I reminded him of the gas chamber waiting at San Quentin Prison.

It was not a good case for a trial lawyer. Chinatown murders rarely are. I was forced to go prospecting. I sauntered into the Homicide Bureau on the fourth floor of the old Hall of Justice, drew up a chair, and began what appeared to be a conversation with myself.

The bureau was humming busily. The telephones were ringing, and policemen were coming and going. A Chinese murder doesn't happen every day. Facing Gariott, I spoke to the wall behind him. "It's a hell of a job, this putting innocent men in jail." No one answered me. "This case is a walkaway." A few heads came up. "It's a funny thing, though, how Tom Yick got two bullets in his precious hide."

"Three," corrected an inspector.

That was better. "Two," I argued. "I don't believe three shots were fired."

"Three shots hit him," the inspector snapped. "Your man emptied his gun and reloaded. Or didn't he tell you that?"

"You found all the bullet holes, I suppose? Or did those dark halls scare you out? I don't believe you even examined that apartment."

"We ransacked the joint!"

I was listening. The police seemed to think more than

one gunload had been fired, though Wong, not a man to lose count of such things, told me he had fired four shots: One was a warning shot, and the next three bullets had hit Yick. If that fourth bullet could be found, I might have a silent witness casting doubt on details of the prosecution's case. I got up. Fishing hadn't been too bad.

Others recalled Wong's wedding ten years before to a big-eyed girl with full red lips and an intriguing figure. She was attractive in either Chinese silks or American frocks, and when she walked, she had a provocative bounce. The police knew Wong befriended Yick. Everyone knew about the love song Yick had sung to Mrs. Wong by name in August while he was working in the Chinese radio station. In fact, the song had gone over two Chinese radio stations.

Wong had complained to his tong. Then he had come to the police and demanded that Yick be driven from Chinatown. The police did warn the singer to keep away from pretty Mrs. Wong. Yick accepted no advice. He was in love.

After the third day of my prowlings, the tong sent a delegation to my office. Three ancients in mandarin costume, with wispy chin whiskers and tiny black caps nodding on their heads, filed in with three young Chinese businessmen. The old gentlemen tucked their hands into voluminous silk sleeves and perched in a semicircle staring at me.

I was familiar with protocol, so I sat wooden-faced in

127

my leather chair and waited. They stared at my huge white cuffs and the gold cuff links. From time to time, without change of expression, they uttered torrents of Cantonese. One of the young men explained that the ancients spoke no English. "What do you think will happen to our brother Mr. Wong?"

"You," I said politely, "Do not believe in the Mosaic Law of an eye for an eye. That is our law. It is a bad law. It makes us practice vengeance rather than compassion. It will be difficult in the case of Mr. Wong. I have no witnesses to prove his innocence or to lower the killing from murder to manslaughter. I have no tools." The Chinese gentlemen bowed and filed out.

A man seeking out secrets in Chinatown by night must not be squeamish. During the late watches, there are creakings in the old buildings, stealthy footsteps that might be cats or might be other men. There are tinkling ornaments, bamboo curtains that rattle, and the mutterings of oldsters dreaming on their hard beds. Foghorns groan from the bay. It was raining a very cold and unfriendly rain that night. Though generally self-assured, I fortified myself with hookers of scotch before I climbed the hill to the house of murder.

No light broke the gloomy face of the old apartment building as I eased through the narrow front door. The stairway creaked. I allowed myself a quick flicker from a pencil flashlight, stepped over the dark red stain to the locked door of Wong's apartment.

Mrs. Wong had gone to live with friends until the trial

was over. Wong was out of harm's way in his cell. There is no bail for Murder I.

As every customer of any of the large life insurance companies knows, around the first of every year the corporations present each of them with a small calendar printed on heavy celluloid. And as every member of the San Francisco police department knows, this calendar's purpose has nothing to do with discovering the day or date. It is used by police and burglars alike for opening spring locks (so-called Yale locks). For this purpose it is superb and possibly superior to even Yale keys. I had just such a calendar in my wallet.

Within three minutes I was inside Wong's apartment with the rain beating briskly on the windows and my heart pounding.

As the police had before, I searched through cabinets, drawers, suitcases, and closets, finding nothing but the things of family life. I passed up Chinese paintings, paper lanterns, and one large ivory statue of some Chinese divinity.

Kneeling, I crawled slowly around the room, using quick flashes to examine the baseboards, where the walls joined the floor of the bedroom. The building was very old, and in one corner the dry old wood of the baseboard had so dried out that the ends didn't quite meet. Between these two ends and implanted in the two-by-four upright I found what I was looking for—one bullet in the old wood.

Keeping the light on the spot, I stood back to gauge

the line of fire. Wong had been truthful. He had fired not three bullets, which the police had from the body, but four. His first shot had hit the two-by-four at an angle. A ballistics specialist would dig out the bullet and identify it. I made a final sweep of the room. The light glinted on the ivory statue, passed it. I suddenly came back.

The off-white statue wore a soft veil of dust, as did its walnut base, but the top was glossy clean. Human hands, it appeared, had lifted the head so many times that a protective film of oil had adhered to it. Something was hidden there. A fat bundle of letters. They were addressed in a man's hand to Mrs. Wong. I jammed them into my pocket.

It was the hardest trial I had ever faced. The patient, trusting young man had done what any husband might do when a predator fouls his nest. But this trial would start on December 18, 1941, just eleven days after Pearl Harbor, and I was defending a man of Oriental birth.

San Franciscans were still in the first shock of war. Honolulu, where their own great fleet lay ruined, seemed only a gull's cry beyond the Golden Gate. There were reports that the conquering Japanese were steaming for California. The blacked-out city shivered.

Justice for a Chinese-American at that moment? People who wouldn't know a Japanese from a Hottentot glared at the chattering citizens of Chinatown, where loyal residents hastily donned lapel buttons proclaiming: "I am Chinese." I felt I might as well have Tojo himself for a client.

I slept poorly and was astir by five each morning, planning, pondering, preparing. I made a careful study of the letters from the Wong apartment. Here, in Yick's own handwriting, was an intimate account of trysts with Wong's wife. Here was startling intelligence. At this very moment, Mrs. Wong was carrying the unborn child of Tom Yick.

I had gone to Los Angeles for a day to find a translator who would have no contact with the San Francisco Chinese. The reason for getting no help for Wong from his wife was now clear. Her refusal to cooperate was justified in her mind.

The homicide inspector was a stern and forceful man who knew his business. He re-created the murder scene and the finding of the body. He said Mrs. Wong was up and dressed because she had been heating milk for one of her babies when the shots were fired.

The medical testimony was blunt. Yick had been hit by three shots at point-blank range: one in the head, two in the chest. Good shooting.

The prosecutor called Mrs. Wong. She appeared almost drab as she minced to the stand. Watching her, I gave particular attention to her figure under the nondescript cloth coat. It held a secret that no one in that room knew but she and I.

It was a quick direct examination. She knew Yick. Her husband was jealous. Yick called, and her husband shot him. Nothing about her relationship with Tom.

On cross-examination I fed her soft, warm leading

131

questions. She shadowboxed. I couldn't dent the armor.

Q. Mrs. Wong [I hesitated, then turned to the counsel table and reached for a large paper envelope], Mrs. Wong, I now call your attention to some letters.

She gasped as the packet spilled onto the table. I continued:

Q. Mrs. Wong, I will now ask you some further questions, and then, maybe, I shall want to ask you about these letters.
A. Yes, sir.

Slowly the reluctant answers came.

Q. When did Tom Yick first call on you and talk to you personally about yourself?
A. It was last year.

I was holding the bundle of letters and occasionally hitting the counsel table with a quiet slap of the packet.

Q. Will you tell Judge Murphy and the ladies and gentlemen of the jury what were the circumstances?
A. One time . . . while my husband was away from home one night . . . he came to make love to me. He touch me . . . and then I said: "You shouldn't do that" . . . and I slapped him on the face . . . and I said, "If you do it again I will tell my husband about it."
Q. Did you see him at any other times?
A. While I was home . . . I caught him several times standing in our fire escape place, and I said: "What are you doing around here, standing over there?" He said: "I want to find out when your husband gets home."
Q. Did he stop coming to see you?
A. No, he still came up.
Q. Did you see Tom Yick often?

She hesitated. I tapped the letters on the table, waiting patiently.

A. Well, he came up to the house often.

Q. Did you tell your husband that Yick was bothering you?

A. Yes, one time . . . I gave him a hint. I said to my husband: "I don't think Tom is a good friend of yours."

Q. When your husband was not in town, did Mr. Yick call on you?

She frowned, crossed her legs, and fumbled nervously at her skirt.

A. Yes.

Q. What were the circumstances?

I was tapping the bundle of letters like a metronome.

A. Well . . . after I told him not to come up . . . he still came up. And one time I was not feeling well. He said he will fix me some tea. So . . . I was drinking the tea . . . and so he made love to me . . . and finally, that night . . . I give in.

Q. Did your husband come home while he was there?

A. He got home, and he found our apartment door was locked, and it took Tom a long time to open it . . . and my husband was mad, and he told Tom not to come up to the house or to his office anymore.

Q. Did he call on you again?

A. Then he came up again a few days later and he said he could not sleep . . . I said, "Why couldn't you sleep?" And he said . . . "Because I miss you very much" . . . And he said, well, he is sick . . . and he said he had written out a song for me, and he said he would sing it on the radio that night . . . and he told me to listen. And so that night on the radio he sang this song.

133

Banging the letters on the counsel table turned the tide. She realized that although I had been referring to them, I had not questioned her, nor had I read their contents to the jury. She knew the father of her unborn child was Tom Yick. Fearing this additional disgrace would be the most devastating, and wanting to save herself even more than saving Wong's life, she blurted out the truth. The cross-examination, in part, continued:

Q. When Yick came to the apartment the last time, was there any conversation before the shooting?

A. They quarreled and said many words, and Tom tried to push my husband out of the apartment.

Q. Push your husband out?

A. Yes, he pushed him out the door, and Tom said, "I will get even with you someday." And then he threatened to kill my husband, and then my husband started shooting.

I asked no more questions. I thanked her. She left the witness stand and quickly and quietly disappeared through the courtroom doors, her secret safe, her emotional turmoil at an end, and her husband's fate in the lap of the jury.

The closing arguments were short and direct. Twenty-three minutes elapsed between the time the jury retired to deliberate Wong's fate and the court clerk's reading the verdict handed him by the jury foreman—NOT GUILTY.

I see Wong occasionally. He is still the same calm, slim, ascetic, neatly dressed gentleman I first met in the Hall of Justice so many, many years ago.

The Billie Holiday Case

THIS is about Billie Holiday, one of America's finest blues singers, who died virtually alone and broke. She became a victim of dope and of society's method of dealing with addicts. When I defended her, she was also the victim of a sometimes equally destructive force called love.

Billie was about at her peak as a blues singer when she was arrested for possession of opium in a hotel in San Francisco, where she was appearing at a nightclub known as Café Society Uptown. The arrest had been made under circumstances which did no credit to due process of law or respect for the Constitution. The way in which Billie was framed recalled to me Jimmie Walker's immortal expression: "There's many a frame that's not around a picture."

Billie was not sharp. She doubted no one. She was a believer. Truth and honesty were as natural for her as was her voice. Billie could not or would not think that

135

sweet talk could be false. She had faith in everyone, particularly and solely her lover, John Levy, whose name was ethnically misleading.

Her fans called her Lady Day, and she spent her five-figure paychecks living up to the title, never thinking that the checks would not be forthcoming someday. She bought clothes and more clothes. Jewelry was a continuing must. Diamonds were her constant investment, but her most expensive investment was in the man market. John Levy was a lover in search of money only. He was her manager. Managers usually take 10 percent of their principals' earnings, but John was a perfectionist—he took it all.

Billie was the dependent type. Once she depended on heroin, and this had finally brought her to the federal reformatory at Alderson, Virginia, where it had taken ten months to rehabilitate her. When she returned to the nightclub circuit more than a year before her San Francisco engagement, she hoped that she was forever through with dope.

During her stay in the reformatory, no real attempt was made to get at the reason for her use of narcotics, so there was no real reason to believe that dope was through with her. However, Billie was clean of the habit when she arrived in San Francisco.

The details of the arrest were interesting and significant.

John Levy and Billie were relaxing in pajamas in their hotel suite when the telephone rang. She took the call.

It was for Levy. He took the receiver and exchanged a few monosyllables with the person on the other end of the line. Later he claimed that someone had asked for a business appointment and that he had agreed to it.

He put down the telephone receiver and handed Billie a small package and told her to flush its contents down the toilet. As she neared the bathroom, there was a sharp rap on the door. Levy, who ostensibly had some personal reason for wanting the package to pass from immediate existence, nevertheless took the promptest action to open the door to the hallway, and in rushed Colonel George White with two San Francisco police inspectors and several of his agents from the Federal Bureau of Narcotics.

The next few seconds in the suite were like a riot. Billie and White arrived at the toilet at about the same time, with Billie flushing and he groping. She had thrown something that was later described as a bottle of opium against the side of the dresser in the course of carrying out Levy's orders. All that the colonel and his men were able to grab from the flushing toilet were a few fragments of glass. One of the fragments contained a brown substance which turned out to be opium when analyzed. Levy and the bewildered Billie were escorted to the Hall of Justice.

It was then that two interesting developments took place: The first was that Colonel White was clearly drawing a bead on Billie, and on Billie only, in his complaint, although Levy was booked, too. Completely disregarding the girl's simple and obviously unimprovised story of what had taken place in the room prior to his entrance—or refusing to believe that the two might at least be equally guilty—White was obviously trying to send Billie and only Billie to prison.

Second, Levy had somehow been exempted from bribery charges despite the fact that the colonel freely stated that the manager tried to bribe him to let Billie go and "forget the incident." "I declined his offer to do that," stated the colonel in describing the incident, apparently momentarily forgetting that offering a bribe to a federal officer is a felony.

The fact that Colonel White would put himself on record as having "declined" the offer was, to me, unrebuttable evidence that White and Levy were partners in the enterprise to dispose of Billie. After all, Levy would want to move freely about New York in the years to come, and Billie had many loyal and often uninhibited admirers in Harlem and elsewhere.

I had before me a dual problem: (1) to defend my client against an apparently ironclad case for the prosecution, and (2) to unframe a frame-up.

Human relationships create trouble, hostility, and strife. These are basic relationships. Where these are concerned, the best man, the best argument, and the best fight will win. But the frame-up and the treachery are outside all rules.

The greatest difficulty was the fact that Billie was still in love with Levy. Not that she didn't entertain even darker suspicions of his character and aims; she merely took the position that no matter what he did to and against her, she still loved him.

I tried to explain to myself why and how she could love the man who was her destroyer but was faced always with a network of facts so minute that my lack of understanding far outweighed my reasoning.

Lady Day in all things acted by compulsion. I realized that here was a soul without a spiritual harbor. She was here, and that was it. Billie was a result. She had not been asked if she would or would not come into the world, nor had she been consulted on the parents she would have. She could not be held accountable for her passion and desire for Levy. These were the result of the temperament which God had given her.

But now was not the time for philosophy. Now was the time for battle.

Meanwhile, Billie was freed on bail and returned to work. This was one case in which publicity provided benefits. The Café was packed nightly.

According to night-life scuttlebutt, Levy had come to the end of the line as far as Billie was concerned; he had been looking around for his nearest exit. He had enough of her money and now owned a Manhattan spot in Harlem called the Club Ebony. He had another girl. But he couldn't just dump Billie. He had his own public image to think about. He had to do something more subtle and conclusive, something that would leave him looking loyal and faithful and appealingly noble.

The transcript of the testimony before the grand jury

was interesting and enlightening. The case was hand-built from the ground up. Colonel White, always super-resourceful, was not content with the official analysis of the brown substance as opium. He supplemented this evidence with an ingenious and creative analysis of the remainder of the broken pipe as an improvised opium pipe. He testified about Levy's attempt to bribe Billie loose, and he made it clear that he had never before had any social, official, commercial, or other contacts with Levy. He testified he knew John Levy by description and reputation, but not by sight. He was not to be prosecuted.

In most cases, all parties—near, over, under, about, or close to a captured drug—are relentlessly prosecuted. Levy was spared this indignity. In some way he endeared himself to the authorities.

Billie in a conference the next morning with me showed evidence of puffiness of one of her eyes, shaded by dark glasses.

As soon as the grand jury had set him free, he had come to the hotel room, beaten her, taken her expensive fur coat, and left for New York.

I talked to her at great length and insisted that she tell the truth about him—to help me show the jury how he put her in this bottomless hole.

She snuffled into her handkerchief before replying.

Her repeated reply was: "I can't do that. I love him."

There are times when love should be grounds for mental commitment.

Billie said she had seen White and Levy together at

the Café Society. The club had a roving camerawoman, and in my judgment John Levy was the type of man who would leave a standing order to snap his picture with every important person who stopped at his table.

I spent hours in her darkroom, poring over hundreds of negatives of every picture she had taken. There it was —a picture of White and Levy seated at the same table. The photographer made a copy for me.

The trial commenced. This prosecutor figured he had an easy one this time. The defendant had a narcotics record. The evidence was chemically authenticated. The principal witness for the prosecution, Colonel White, was a cool and knowledgeable expert, resourceful under cross-examination, famed and popular as a dope fighter. The prosecutor had already cut a notch in his briefcase for this one. Even White, a man not prone to count chickens that were still in their shells, was wearing the tight little smile of a man who had already heard the jury's verdict and liked it.

The opening statement of the prosecutor was a flawless indictment; it put Billie in a prison cell. Colonel White then turned the key in the lock with a cool businesslike piece of testimony that was straight from the manual.

I questioned White whether it was the practice of a federal officer to bypass the need for a warrant in making a raid by taking a city policeman along. (City police, at that time could break and enter a premise, warrantless, merely on their hunch that a felony was being committed.) The prosecutor promptly objected, but the jury had heard the question and was deprived of hearing the answer which—had it been handled skillfully—would have made White's raid look far better than it did.

White was then asked how long he'd known John Levy. He said, "Since the arrest." Had he met Levy at any time previously? He said, "Never!" Had he and Levy ever discussed the way to carry out the raid? "No!" By now the jurors were looking at Colonel White with new interest. They were beginning to wonder if they were not being given *some* of the truth, carefully *chosen* truth, and only *as much of the truth* as someone regarded as good for them.

The cross-examination commenced:

Q. Mr. White, you are in charge of federal narcotics law enforcement?

A. Yes.

Q. You are not a police officer in the city and county of San Francisco?

A. No.

Q. Is it your habit and custom to make arrests for the purpose of turning the case over to the state authorities for prosecution?

A. No.

Q. Have you followed the practice of making arrests as a federal agent and referring the case to the state authorities?

The court sustained an objection, but the jury was beginning to get the idea.

Q. How long have you known John Levy?

A. Since January 22, 1949.

142

Q. Did you know him at any other time?

A. No.

Q. Were you and he friends?

A. No.

Q. Did you and he visit together?

A. At what time are you referring to?

Q. At any time?

A. Subsequent to his arrest I had several conversations with him.

Q. About what?

An objection was sustained.

Q. Isn't it a fact that, as the result of what Levy told you, you entered the hotel on the day of the arrest?

A. No. It is not a fact!

Q. Isn't it a fact that Levy is the man who got in touch with you and gave you information as a result of which you went to this hotel?

A. That is not correct.

Q. Well, isn't it a fact that you dismissed the charge against Levy?

Again an objection was sustained.

Q. Let's put it this way: Isn't it a fact that you were in court when the case against Levy was dismissed?

A. No, sir, it is not a fact. I was not there.

Q. When you arrived at Miss Holiday's apartment, how did you gain admittance?

A. I knocked on the door and said I was the manager. In about fifteen seconds the door opened and I entered.

Q. Who opened the door?

A. John Levy.

Q. Did you know Levy at that time?

A. No, sir. I knew him by description and reputation, *but not by sight*.

Q. When did you first see Miss Holiday?

A. I first saw Billie Holiday when she was listening at the door. I told her I was a narcotics agent. She turned and ran toward the bathroom. I followed.

Q. Did you run, walk, or—

A. I ran. She threw herself down over the open toilet bowl, at the same time taking the object she had in her hand, a blackened bottle, and smashing it on the edge. She pulled the flush rod with her left hand. [White was explaining the evidence he had collected.] This represents an improvised opium pipe. It is what we retrieved from the floor of the bathroom. This is a small glass medicine bottle which has been made into an opium pipe and used for the purpose of smoking opium. This is an eye-dropper which appears to contain traces of opium.

Q. Did you question Miss Holiday?

A. Aside from admitting her identity, she had nothing to say.

Q. Did you at that time question Levy?

A. Yes. Levy said to me: "What do you have on this girl?" I said, "We have possession of opium and an opium pipe." Levy said, "I can't believe it." He asked if he could speak to me alone. I asked the others to leave. Levy then asked me if it couldn't be fixed up, and I asked what he meant. He said he meant to pay me some money. I said he couldn't fix it in that fashion. Levy then told me he was acquainted with narcotics agents in New York City and mentioned their names and said he had cooperated with these agents by furnishing information on previous occasions in years gone by and said he would be able to telephone people and have them deliver a quantity of opium or heroin to San Francisco so I could apprehend them. I declined his offer to do that.

Q. You knew Mr. Levy by reputation?

A. Yes.

Q. And you knew by his reputation that he was and is an informer?

The question and answer, of course, were stricken.

Q. And what was the occasion of your knowing him *by reputation?*

A. I first heard of Levy while I was working in New York in about 1941.

Q. Did Levy offer you a bribe?

A. No.

Q. Did you accept the bribe?

A. No.

Q. Did you arrest him for offering you a bribe?

A. No.

Q. Did you ever charge him with offering you a bribe?

A. No.

Q. Isn't it a fact that you and Levy discussed what you wanted Levy to say to Miss Holiday and you called her in and had him say it to her? Isn't that a fact?

A. No.

Q. Isn't it a fact that you knew, or that Levy told you, that he was trying to get rid of Billie Holiday because he had promised to marry her?

A. No.

Q. Didn't he tell you in that conversation he was trying to get rid of Billie Holiday?

A. At no time.

Q. Mr. Levy is in New York right now?

A. I don't know.

Q. You know he is not here.

A. I don't know.

Before concluding the cross-examination it was imperative that the jury know about the existence of the picture of Levy and White. I believed it certain that the court would not permit the introduction of the photograph, but it was necessary to call attention to its existence.

In my judgment nothing was more damaging to the prosecution than to introduce evidence of the closeness of White and Levy. This picture could turn the tide in Billie Holiday's favor and would firmly establish in the minds of the jury that she was framed by Levy.

The cross-examination continued:

Q. I show you a photograph and ask whether it is a photograph of you and John Levy?

One of the jurors stretched to look. Colonel White reached for the photograph.

The witness and the cross-examiner were bending over the photo together. There was a chuckle and the judge warned: "Let's not have a conversation between you and the witness."

I gazed blandly at the bench. "It so happens this time I am not guilty, Your Honor. I didn't say anything; the witness spoke to me. He merely said that it was not a good picture of him."

The closing arguments were superfluous. The jury was out for two and a half hours. Billie was still scared, still ready to cry as the foreman reported the verdict: not guilty!

The jury foreman was talking to the press. They had taken two ballots, he revealed. The jury believed the defense contention that she was framed.

Billie had been unframed.

Billie Holiday sings no more.

Narcotic addiction is an illness—not a crime. Whether the medical profession can discover a cure, certainly imprisonment is not the answer.

We are caring for our fellow humans: the poor and the sick. We do not put them in the hands of the police and jailers. But we have not yet reached the point of enlightenment where we want to help the addict.

Billie Holiday is dead.

The Poor Witness

THE defendant in a criminal case, in implementation of his constitutional right to have compulsory process to obtain witnesses to testify in his behalf, has the right to interview the witnesses who may be called by the prosecution as a matter of due process of law.

So concerned is the law for due process that prosecuting officers, police, and sheriffs may not interfere with this right by ordering witnesses not to talk to defendants or their counsel.

It is a criminal offense willfully to prevent or dissuade a person who is or may become a witness from attending a trial, or to give or offer a bribe to a witness or one about to be called as a witness on the understanding that his testimony will be thereby influenced or that he will not attend a trial, or to procure another person to commit perjury.

The unlawful detention of a witness, under some circumstances, is punishable as a contempt of court.

Competent people who are present in court, including parties to an action, may, with certain exceptions, be required to answer legal questions that are pertinent to the matter in issue, though the answers may establish a claim against those testifying.

This rule also applies to expert witnesses. When such an expert has made the necessary investigation and formed an opinion, he may be required to testify to that opinion, but a party cannot impose on an unwilling witness the duty of going to the trouble of making a scientific investigation in order that he may form and give an expert opinion.

The witness may be compelled by the court to answer questions, and a recalcitrant witness may be punished for contempt.

It must be borne in mind that a party to the litigation or a witness has a constitutional right to be free from unreasonable searches and seizures. For example: Though there is no absolute privilege to decline to reveal a trade secret, as may be the case where certain confidential relationships exist, nevertheless, unless the rights of innocent people are dependent on disclosure, the property right of the possessor of a trade secret is protected. However, no privilege of secrecy is recognized if the rights of possible innocent people depend essentially or chiefly for this ascertainment on the disclosure in question.

A witness who has been subpoenaed to bring certain documents into court may refuse to discuss the case with the attorneys for either side or to exhibit to them the subpoenaed documents, and the fact of such a refusal cannot be brought out on his examination.

A witness need not give an answer that will have a direct tendency to degrade his character, unless it be to the very fact in issue or to a fact from which the fact in issue would be presumed. The privilege afforded by this rule is personal to the witness and has no application to questions addressed to other people.

The court must pass on the sufficiency of the witness' objection to answering. And when the question is innocent in form but some possible answer might tend to degrade, the witness must make it appear to the court that his answer might have such a tendency.

The Howl *Case*

❧—❧

THE defendant was charged with a violation of the Penal Code of the State of California. The complaint alleged that he did willfully and lewdly print, publish, and sell obscene and indecent writings, papers, and books—to wit, *Howl and Other Poems.*

The statute requires proof of criminal intent—namely, that the defendant did willfully and lewdly commit the alleged crime.

It must be borne in mind that the prosecution had the burden of proving beyond a reasonable doubt and to a moral certainty two things: first, that the book was obscene and, second, that the defendant willfully and lewdly committed the crime charged.

It is elementary that when a statute makes a specific intent an element of an offense, such intent must be proved. The proof may be circumstantial, but if so, the circumstances must be such as reasonably to justify an inference of the intent.

The evidence showed that *Howl* was published by the defendant, and therefore it remained to be seen whether the poem was obscene and, if so, whether the defendant had willfully and lewdly published it.

The prosecution contended that having published the poem, the defendant had knowledge of the character of its contents and that from such knowledge a lewd intent might be inferred.

Over the objection of the prosecution, the defense produced nine expert witnesses, some of them with outstanding qualifications in the literary field.

All the defense experts agreed that *Howl* had literary merit, that it represented a sincere effort by the author to present a social picture, and that the language used was relevant to the theme. As Professor Mark Schorer (University of California) put it: *"Howl,* like any work of literature, attempts and intends to make a significant comment on, or interpretation of, human experience as the author knows it."

The prosecution produced two experts in rebuttal, whose qualifications were less than those of the defense. One testified that *Howl* had some clarity of thought but was an imitation of Walt Whitman and had no literary merit; the other and by far the more voluble, that it had no value at all.

It is difficult to believe that in a world so full of temptations as this, any gentleman, whose life would have been virtuous if he had not read Aristophanes and Juvenal, would have been made vicious by reading them.

There is no known record of anyone who said obscene or indecent writings did *him* any harm. They always say it's protecting somebody else, but no one has ever met the people they're protecting.

There is little or no evidence that so-called obscenity has any adverse effect on people. To say that reading a book would provoke someone to rape seems ridiculous. Pull down the bars and filth will sink to its own level.

If *Howl* had been banned it would have been a disgrace to the American intelligence, and *Howl* would have joined a long historic list of banned books, including Homer's *Odyssey,* Cervantes' *Don Quixote,* Defoe's *Robinson Crusoe,* Swift's *Gulliver's Travels,* Goethe's *Faust,* Whitman's *Leaves of Grass,* Hawthorne's *Scarlet Letter,* and the Holy Scriptures.

It is ironic that the suppressed books of one age, in many cases, become part of the accepted literature or even the venerated classics of the next.

Direct examination by Mr. Ralph McIntosh.

Q. Will you state your name, sir?

A. John Bley.

Q. And where do you live?

A. 1021 Menlo Oaks Drive, Menlo Park.

Q. What is your business or occupation at the present?

A. I am an assistant professor of English at the University of San Francisco.

Q. How long have you been so employed?

A. I am in my eighth year.

Q. And previous to that time did you have some connection with Stanford?

A. I was an assistant instructor at Stanford, yes.

Q. For how long?

A. About two and a half years.

Q. And you are presently taking some work there at Stanford?

A. Yes, I'm finishing my PhD degree at Stanford.

Q. And have you also written, published poetry at times?

A. On occasion in the past I have published some poetry, yes.

Q. Now, at my request you have looked at People's No. One in Evidence, the edition called *Howl and Other Poems* by Allen Ginsberg?

A. I have.

Q. And have you formed an opinion, sir, about whether or not that publication has any literary value?

A. I formed an opinion. It's my opinion that if it has any literary value, it is negligible.

Q. Negligible. Can you explain that to us, Mr. Bley, how you arrived at that opinion?

A. There are many bases for criticism, of course, subjective and objective. I endeavored to arrive at my opinion on an objective basis. For example, a great literary work, or even fairly great literary work, would obviously be exceedingly successful in form, but this poem is really just a weak imitation of a form that was used eighty to ninety years ago by Walt Whitman, imitation.

Q. Do you recall the title of that poem?

A. *Leaves of Grass* would be the name of the poem. Literary value could also reside in theme, and what little literary value there is in *Howl* it seems to me does come in theme. The statement of the idea of the poem was relatively clear, but it has little validity, and, therefore, the theme has a negative value, no value at all.

The third basis of objective criticism would be the— well, what for lack of a better term, I would call opportunity. The poet or the writer and his time and his problems—pardon me—the problems of the time, should have some kind of significant interaction. This poem is apparently dedicated to a long-dead movement—Dadaism —and some late followers of Dadaism. And therefore, the opportunity is long past for any significant literary contribution of this poem. Those are my objective bases.

Mr. McIntosh: All right. You may cross-examine.

Cross-Examination by Mr. Ehrlich.

Q. You have done some writing?

A. In a small way, yes.

Q. Have you studied literature generally?

A. Yes, the last ten years of my life have been spent in that.

Q. In what field?

A. My specialty is the English novel. I have concentrated, however, on all English literature from 1660 to date and do teach courses in such works.

Q. What subject did you teach?

A. Well, I taught freshman English and engineering English and narration during that period.

Q. You set out three bases which you use as guides in your evaluation of poetic works, is that right?

A. Yes, my objective bases.

Q. Do you apply those three bases to your evaluation of every poetic work?

A. Yes, that is my consistent objective aim.

Q. Have you had occasion to review poetry for the reading public?

A. Oh, for publication, no.

Q. Are your three bases accepted by men who are critics of poetry?

A. Doubtless they are accepted by some critics of poetry because they are fairly standard rules.

Q. Some accept, and some do not.

A. That's right.

155

Q. Did I understand you to say that Ginsberg used the Walt Whitman style?

A. The form, the form of the book *Leaves of Grass*.

Q. Ginsberg used the same format or form—is that what you are saying?

A. That's right.

Q. And because of Ginsberg's using that format, it is your opinion that the poem *Howl* has no literary value or merit?

A. On the basis of form, that is correct, because great literature always creates its own form for each significant occasion.

Q. By that you do not mean that Walt Whitman's *Leaves of Grass* doesn't quite qualify?

A. That is great literature; the form was created by Walt Whitman.

Q. And it is great literature?

A. Right.

Q. And that form is a great form?

A. For Walt Whitman and on that occasion.

Q. At the same time you say that because Ginsberg copied that format, *Howl* has no value or merit, is that correct, sir?

A. That is correct. An imitation never does have the value of the original.

Q. Have you ever imitated another's style, Mr. Bley?

A. In forming what little style I have, of course I have. Every student in trying to form his own style obviously begins on a basis of imitation, not of just one writer, but of many writers.

Q. Well, then, in your opinion, it is good to imitate, isn't it?

A. As a student exercise, yes.

Q. Whom did Walt Whitman copy?

A. To my knowledge, no one.

Q. You don't know, isn't that your answer?

A. That's right.

Q. I understand your next signpost to be that the idea of *Howl* is clear but has little validity?

A. That is the general conclusion, yes, in theme; the idea of *Howl* is clear in theme.

Q. Please explain that to me, if you will. The idea is good, we agree on that, do we?

A. The idea is clear.

Q. What is Ginsberg's idea in *Howl*?

A. Well, he celebrates the unfortunate life of—I can't remember the man's name—Solomon—the unfortunate life of the man, Solomon, who is a drifter of Dadaist persuasion.

Q. He portrays that?

A. That's correct.

Q. And does that portrayal have any validity?

A. Not as literature, no.

Q. Let's take one step at a time. Is there any validity in the story Ginsberg is telling?

A. A representation of Solomon's life. I take it on faith that it must be a valid, true picture.

Q. And when Ginsberg goes a little bit further and condemns this existence, which has soured and engulfed Solomon, that too is a valid description of what Ginsberg feels, is that right?

A. I am sorry, but I didn't identify any condemnation.

Q. Well, let's put it your way. This sympathy which Ginsberg shows for Solomon, would you say that it is honestly portrayed?

A. As an individual writer, yes.

Q. What is your impression and your understanding of it?

A. My understanding there would be based on a reference to the value, the value statement of the third portion, wherein the poet expresses the usual Dadaist line that everything is created for man's despair and everything must be forgotten and destroyed and that Solomon's life apparently has had this kind of rhythm. Therefore, there is some validity of theme, you see, in that area.

Q. Then there is validity of theme?

A. As a Dadaist statement, yes.

Q. Well, I don't care what qualifications you put on it, but there is validity in Ginsberg's theme, isn't there?

A. Well, I am afraid that I have got my tongue tripped up here—this clarity—I should have said—clarity instead of validity.

Q. But you have been using the term "validity" all the time you have been on the stand. By the way, Mr. Bley, have you read the Holy Bible?

A. I have.

Q. You don't know who wrote Job, do you?

A. I am sure I didn't.

Q. Now tell me, did you read Job?

A. I have.

Q. Will you agree with me that Job does condemn life?

A. Not to the same end that the Dadaist does, no.

Q. Let's leave the Dadaist out. Just stick with Job for a moment. Doesn't Job condemn the position of man's fortune on earth?

Mr. McIntosh: I will object to any comparison with the Bible, Your Honor, as to what Job said.

The court: No. The witness stated that he didn't know of any particular example of any writer in the same vein, and he stated that he has read Job, and that Job, I presume, counsel is going to show that Job does cover the same theme in somewhat the same way. I don't know whether—

Mr. Ehrlich: That is right.

The court: I think that is what he is driving at. So I will overrule the objection. Mr. Bley, so that you won't

158

be confused, that requires a yes or no answer, and you may explain your answer after you have answered. In other words, you are not confined to a yes or no answer.

The witness: Job does condemn man's condition, then yes, but he does not go on then, as the Dadaist goes on, to desire to wipe out all memory of the past, to wipe out all human memory of everything that the human race has ever done so that there can be a fresh start made, as the Dadaist does.

Mr. Ehrlich: And that's one of the reasons why you think *Howl* has no validity, because it wants to wipe out everything and start over, is that it?

A. Well, no. That was the only small validity that I found in *Howl* because that gives it some literary merit, some message of some sort.

Q. Mr. Bley, I am quoting from Job in the Holy Bible:

When shall I arise, and the night be gone? and I am full of tossings to and fro unto the dawning of the day.

My flesh is clothed with worms and clods of dust; my skin is broken, and become loathsome.

My days are swifter than a weaver's shuttle, and are spent without hope. . . .

Therefore I will not refrain my mouth; I will speak in the anguish of my spirit; I will complain in the bitterness of my soul. . . .

When I say, My bed shall comfort me, my couch shall ease my complaint;

Then thou scarest me with dreams, and terrifiest me through visions:

So that my soul chooseth strangling, and death rather than my life.

I loathe it; I would not live alway, let me alone; for my days are vanity. . . .

I have sinned; what shall I do unto thee, O thou

preserver of men? Why hast thou set me as a mark against thee, so that I am a burden to myself?

And why dost thou not pardon my transgression, and take away my iniquity? for now shall I sleep in the dust; and thou shalt seek me in the morning, but I shall not be.

Isn't Job condemning the futility of life as Ginsberg condemns the futility of life?

A. Not at all. Job may be condemning the suffering of his own life, futility of his own life, but he is not condemning anything that's being talked about in *Howl*.

Q. Well, what is Ginsberg doing with Solomon? Isn't he doing the same thing, only speaking in the third person?

A. I found no air of condemnation in the poem at all.

Q. What is the Dadaist aim to which you referred earlier?

A. Well, as a literary movement about 1918 to 1921, this group of French writers decided that the world was in such a mess that the only hope for the world was to destroy all memory of everything that men had ever accomplished through history, that each individual should destroy all memory of everything that ever happened to him, that language and communications should be destroyed, and then on that basis perhaps a fresh start toward a better world might be made. That is a generalization of the Dadaist theme.

Q. In your opinion, that is what Ginsberg has tried to do, is that right, sir?

A. As he portrays the life of Solomon, who is identified as a Dadaist, and shows sympathy with Solomon, who is identified as a Dadaist, he seems to indicate that he has a friendship toward that idea, yes.

Q. And you don't believe in that philosophy, do you?

A. Not at all. It has been dead since about 1922 or '23, when the followers moved into the area of Surrealism almost unanimously.

Q. That does not necessarily mean that a person who thinks as a Dadaist is wrong, does it?

A. No, but that does not create literature.

Q. Well, what creates literature, Mr. Bley?

A. I'd have to return to my three bases for an objective criticism.

Q. Those three you gave?

A. Form, theme, and opportunity.

Q. Well, let's get to the third one, then. Your third point is opportunity, sir?

A. That is correct.

Q. And when you say "opportunity," you mean what, with relation to the matter here?

A. Well, as I first said, the word "opportunity" I inserted for the want of a better word. It means the correlation of the poet and his ideas with his time and with all times. Great pieces of literature appear with a definite message and application to the problems of the particular time in which they appear, and if they are great pieces of literature, they continue to have this validity and they continue to have a message. There is opportunity.

Q. Do you think that Ginsberg in his travels had the opportunity to observe life and to write about it?

A. A small segment, yes.

Q. And this is the segment he is writing about, is that not true?

A. One thing—

Q. Answer that, yes or no, please.

A. I am confused.

Q. This is the segment he is writing about, isn't that right, sir?

A. I can't answer that either yes or no.

Q. You say that in his travels he wrote about a small segment of what?

A. Here is where the confusion comes in: I believe the travels are Solomon's, isn't that right?

Q. What is that, please?

A. I believe the travels are Solomon's, not Ginsberg's. That is the basis of my confusion.

Q. Well, Ginsberg is writing about Solomon; it's his own observations. You have read that, haven't you?

A. Yes.

Q. All right. You know Ginsberg wrote about it, don't you?

A. Know that he wrote the poem, yes.

Q. And you know in Solomon he is depicting his own travels?

A. No, I do not know that.

Q. He is depicting the travels of someone else?

A. That seems to me—

Q. And watches them? He's watching the travels of this man Solomon, and he is describing them, isn't that right?

A. That is what appears to be there, yes.

Q. Yes. Now, he had the opportunity to do so, isn't that right?

A. What is the antecedent to he?

Q. Ginsberg.

A. Ginsberg. I don't know.

Q. Then, not knowing, you are unable to form an opinion as to whether he did or did not have the opportunity to write this?

A. I am unable to know whether he has an acquaintance with Solomon. That is the thing beyond my experience, beyond my knowledge.

Q. Well, let me ask you, Mr. Bley, whether you know Ginsberg or Solomon or whether or not Ginsberg knew Solomon—we're talking about this work and about the impression you get of this work, and your answer now is that you don't know whether Ginsberg knows Solomon.

A. That is correct.

162

Q. Do you evaluate a work by knowing whether the writer knew the person he is talking about?

A. Absolutely.

Q. In *Vanity Fair* was Becky Sharp a personal friend of Thackeray?

A. I don't think so, no.

Q. Well, will you say that *Vanity Fair* is one of the great works of literature?

A. That is correct.

Q. And you don't know—

A. I am certain Becky Sharp never lived as an individual, if that's what you are driving at.

Q. Are you certain that Solomon never lived?

A. No.

Q. Then you don't know, do you?

A. Not at all.

Q. So that your former answer that you couldn't answer my question whether Ginsberg was properly describing Solomon's life is that you do not know whether Ginsberg knew Solomon and, therefore, you couldn't tell whether he was properly describing it?

A. I didn't say that I did not know Solomon; I said that I did not know if he knew Solomon.

Q. Let's go back to Becky Sharp and *Vanity Fair*. Did Becky Sharp know the author?

A. That is a frivolous question.

Q. Is that a frivolous question?

A. Yes.

Mr. McIntosh: Already asked and answered, too.

Mr. Ehrlich: Every question is frivolous when he can't answer it.

Mr. McIntosh: I will object to these scurrilous remarks.

Mr. Ehrlich: Whether it is scurrilous or not, he can't answer the question.

The court: All right, gentlemen. Next question.

Mr. Ehrlich: Well, a lot of books have been written

over the years depicting life as the writer saw it. That's generally true, isn't it, sir?

A. I am under that impression.

Q. Have you read or heard of Gerhard Gerhards?

A. No.

Q. Have you read or heard of Desiderius Erasmus?

A. I have.

Q. Erasmus was a distinguished writer, wasn't he?

A. I have little acquaintance with Erasmus. My study begins with 1660.

Q. 1660. You wouldn't dare to go back a day before 1660, would you?

Mr. McIntosh: Object to that, Your Honor.

The court: The objection is sustained, Mr. Ehrlich.

Mr. Ehrlich: Well, let me tell you about Erasmus. Maybe you did read him and have forgotten. He wrote a great deal—

Mr. McIntosh: I'll object to that type of question, Your Honor, telling him a story and then going to ask him a question on it.

Mr. Ehrlich: Let me tell him about Erasmus. He says he doesn't know anything about Erasmus, just heard about him. As I understand, he wasn't acquainted with—

The court: Let me hear the question.

Mr. Ehrlich: Erasmus did a great deal of writing, and one of his writings which has come down to us through the years is a work titled *The Praise of Folly*. Do you recall reading that?

A. I have never read it.

Q. Have you read anything by François Arouet?

A. No, sir.

Q. Have you read Voltaire?

A. I read one work—*Candide*.

Q. What is your opinion of *Candide?*

A. It is great literature.

Q. When you say "great literature," you mean what?

A. I'd have to return to the three bases again for objective criticism: form, theme, opportunity.

Q. He copied Walt Whitman's style, is that right?

A. Not Voltaire, no.

Q. Whose style did Voltaire copy?

A. I do not know enough about French stylists and French forms to answer that. I have read the work only in translation.

Q. So there is some qualification to style copying to which you originally referred?

A. I don't see there is. No.

Mr. McIntosh: Oh—

Mr. Ehrlich: Please.

The court: Well, counsel has a right to make an objection.

Mr. Ehrlich: If he objects.

Mr. McIntosh: I would like to. I didn't want to box with him; he's disturbing me. I get my mouth open and out fly fists.

Mr. Ehrlich: Well now, going back to Voltaire, and the only thing you read written by Voltaire—by the way, you know how much he wrote, don't you?

A. I have a general idea.

Q. Safe to say that he wrote on hundreds of subjects, didn't he?

A. Without a doubt.

Q. Now, getting back to *Candide,* would you say that Voltaire had the idea of *Candide* as a clear-cut idea?

A. That's not my recollection of it, no. It took some little reflection to get at an approximation of the idea.

Q. Well, did you feel that there was any validity in the nature and character of his work?

A. That's the memory I have of *Candide,* yes.

Q. Well, if you had difficulty in understanding what Voltaire's idea was, how can you come to the conclusion

—or give us your reason for coming to the conclusion that it had validity?

A.   Upon the basis of reflection.

Q.   What was your reflection?

A.   Well, I am afraid it's been ten or twelve years since I read this. The pattern of reflection would be difficult to recall. My identification as a valid theme would not come immediately upon reading *Candide*, only upon reflection.

Q.   How long have you reflected on *Howl?*

A.   Let's see. What is the date?

The court: Today is the nineteenth of September.

The Witness: Nineteenth. I believe two weeks.

Mr. Ehrlich: Two weeks?

A.   Two weeks would be the limit of my opportunity. However, I made up my mind after five minutes.

Q.   Two weeks was the limit of your opportunity. And you reflected for a long, long time on Voltaire's *Candide*, is that right?

A.   Exactly. A great work of literature frequently conveys all kinds of challenges.

Q.   Well, do you believe that if you reflected for another ten years on *Howl,* you might change your opinion?

A.   I am quite certain I would not.

Q.   You are quite certain today that you will not change your mind in the next ten years, is that right, sir?

A.   That is correct.

Mr. Ehrlich: Step down.

It would have been a basic mistake to cross-examine the chief prosecution witness Bley in an effort to force him to change his opinion of *Howl*. It is reasonable to believe he would not change his testimony given on direct examination from which it appeared that he was determined that there was no literary value, merit, or other value in Ginsberg's poem. Bley was biased.

In a situation of this kind, it was essential to show that the witness had little or no basis for his opinion. To do this, the trial lawyer must not attack the opinion but must carefully cross-examine on related subjects. This course brought to the attention of the judge the fact that the witness was not qualified to render an opinion favorable or unfavorable to *Howl* or its author.

A careful reading of Bley's direct examination and the cross-examination illustrates how this was accomplished. His testimony on direct examination was completely destroyed. The court at the conclusion of the trial based its findings and decision on the failure of Bley to qualify as a literary expert, saying in effect that Bley's testimony was biased and based on little, if any, learning, knowledge, or experience.

It became apparent during the cross-examination that Bley was on the stand for the purpose solely of denouncing the poem. His educational background showed that he was not the intellectual scholar he represented himself to be on his direct examination. On cross-examination it became apparent that his knowledge of literature was limited.

When questioned whether he had read any of the works of Gerhard Gerhards, he said he had not. When asked if he had read Erasmus, he answered affirmatively. This immediately brought to the judge's mind that Bley did not know that Gerhards and Desiderius Erasmus were one and the same man. In fact, it was clear that he knew nothing of this famous Dutch theologian and writer.

When questioned on cross-examination whether he had read or knew anything about François Arouet, he answered no, and when asked if he had read any of the works of Voltaire, his affirmative answer immediately told the court that Bley's educational background was limited; François Arouet and Voltaire were one and the same person.

Had he studied literature from 1660 as he testified, he would have known that Voltaire was the most famous, the best loved, and the most hated man of his time. Voltaire rebelled against the iniquities of his class. His life was shaped by the horrors of injustice. He challenged Christianity, the church, the king, and the courts. He was an indefatigable writer. The long list of his productions embraces works in almost every branch of literature— poetry, drama, romance, history, philosophy, criticism— and even science.

The Ryan Case

THE defendant James J. Ryan was charged with voluntary manslaughter.

Manslaughter can be of several kinds. There is a voluntary manslaughter, which is an intentional killing upon a sudden quarrel or in a heat of passion.

On the day of the shooting, Ryan and Robert Gillian, —both of whom were police officers, were off duty. They had arranged a trip to Lake Misser. Robert Gillian dated a girl named Bonnie Kruzek, and Ryan dated Nancy Ottler.

On the trip back to town the group made a number of stops, anywhere from five to ten, during which the testimony showed that Ryan drank wine from a full gallon jug to the point at which there was about an inch and a half or two inches of wine left in the bottom.

During the ride home there was an argument between Ryan and Nancy Ottler because of her inattentiveness to him, and at one point she said to him that he smelled bad from drinking too much wine.

As they approached town, about six o'clock in the evening, they drove into Clavel Court, where Gillian kept his boat. Dark was approaching, and as they brought the boat into Clavel Court, they drove up the center of the court, where they parked the car and boat trailer.

At that time both Gillian and Ryan got out of the car, leaving the doors ajar, and opened the trunk of the automobile, apparently looking, among other things, for Gillian's gun. At about this time a Charles Rudd, a black man, came along in his automobile. The testimony showed that he and Mrs. Rudd live on Clavel Court, at its very dead end.

When Mr. and Mrs. Rudd drove into Clavel Court, he followed his habit of backing his car into the end of the court. Because of the size of the street there, it was much easier to back in and then leave by driving forward in the morning.

On this occasion he observed the boat and trailer, and he started to back his car in. The car and trailer were blocking the center of the street, so he attempted to drive up on the sidewalk and back around the side of the car when one of his fenders scraped the fender on the boat trailer.

There was a slight bump, but no significant damage to either car. At best there was a transfer of paint from one vehicle to the other. There were no dented fenders. But at this moment Ryan yelled: "Stop it; you hit my trailer!" Rudd got out of his car, which he had moved

forward, and came back and said: "Well, you are blocking the street and I thought I could get by. I didn't make
it."

Ryan said: "If you move your car and hit my trailer,
I'll shoot you."

Mrs. Rudd, who was riding with her husband, also
alighted from the car, and she came over to where Ryan
and her husband were. Rudd was saying: "Well, there
isn't any damage anyway." There was some discussion
about the insurance companies who would have to pay.
Rudd finally said: "Well, call the police and we will set-
tle the matter."

Mr. Rudd, receiving no response to this, said, "I will
go and call the police," and began to walk toward the
dead end of the court where he lived. Ryan then grabbed
him and shoved him against a pole and said, "If you
leave, it will be a hit-and-run accident—let me see your
driver's license."

At this Mrs. Rudd became excited and said, "You
don't have to show him your driver's license." She immediately left the scene and went to her home at the
blind end of Clavel Court.

Rudd did in fact give his driver's license to Ryan, who
sat himself partially inside his car with his legs extended
out and began to write Rudd's identification.

Mrs. Rudd had gone to her house, where her son by
a previous marriage, Ray Dunhill, was taking a coffee
break from driving his truck, as she knew from seeing
the truck parked in the court. She told Dunhill: "Your

stepdad is having some trouble down on the street, and I am going to call the police."

Dunhill then left and went into the street to find out what the trouble was. When he arrived, he saw Ryan sitting in the passenger's side of his automobile, Charles Rudd, his stepfather, standing alongside. He directed his words to Mr. Rudd: "What happened; what's the matter?"

Up to this time neither Ryan nor Gillian had in any manner identified themselves as police officers, and they were not known by those living in the court as police officers.

About this time, Mrs. Rudd came back down onto the landing of her house at the end of the court, and there was a shot. Ryan jumped from where he was seated and took out his gun, pointed it up to the end of the court yelling, "Drop it; drop it," and fired one shot toward her.

Rudd testified he was standing outside the car. Meanwhile, his wife had gone into their house: "When she returned, Ryan came out of his car with a pistol in his hand and told my wife to drop it, or I'll shoot. He assumed that my wife had a gun."

Ryan testified that he saw the gun in Mrs. Rudd's hand when she fired at him. He said it was a blue metal revolver.

Ray Dunhill, who was standing there and saw his mother at the end of the court, ran and tackled Ryan, knocking him down. During the tussle, Ryan's gun fell to the street. About the same time Ray Dunhill was jumped on by Gillian and knocked to the ground. During this struggle, Dunhill kicked the gun away from Ryan.

About this time, hearing what sounded like gunshots, Special Police Officer Abe Zedd drove his patrol car to Clavel Court. At the entrance of the court he was met by Gillian, who identified himself as a police officer and requested a gun, which Zedd gave him.

As they returned to the center of the court, Ryan was on the ground, and several people were struggling with him.

Ryan finally recovered his gun from the place where it had fallen when Ray Dunhill knocked him down.

Police Officers Ryan and Gillian and Special Officer Zedd got Rudd, Dunhill, and Glen Bertram, who had arrived during the struggle, placed against a wall with their hands and legs spread-eagled.

Everything was quiet, so Special Officer Zedd went to where his car was parked to move it nearer to Clavel Court.

When he returned, he saw that Glen Bertram had moved from the wall and picked up a heavy stick, which was twenty-three inches long. He and Ryan began circling each other, Ryan pointing the gun at Glen Bertram and the latter trying to hit Ryan with the stick. Ryan was saying he was going to shoot Bertram if he didn't put the stick down.

173

Bertram swung at the gun, swung at Ryan, and struck Ryan on the elbow and on the side of the head. Ryan fired, shooting Bertram in the upper chest, killing him.

In California a criminal defendant, on his first appearance in court, is given a copy of the transcript of testimony heard by the grand jury which returned the indictment charging him with the crime.

It was clear from reading the Ryan transcript that the girls who accompanied the two off-duty policemen to Lake Misser would testify at the trial that Ryan drank the most part of a gallon of red wine. The prosecution hoped to convince the trial jury that at the time of the shooting, Ryan was under the influence of alcohol, and because voluntary intoxication is not a defense, he was guilty of willfully killing Bertram.

Thus it became necessary to prepare a reasonable response to such testimony. When Dunhill came under cross-examination, he opened the way to destroy the girl's testimony of intoxication. Bear in mind that Dunhill wrestled with Ryan and pushed or threw the defendant to the ground with such force that Ryan lost possession of his gun. The testimony about wrestling with Ryan was the foundation for the important questions about Ryan's sobriety.

The cross-examination would have to exonerate Ryan completely of the killing charge, as well as destroy the wine-drinking gambit.

The direct examination commenced:

Portion of the Direct Cross-Examination

Q. All right. Do you recognize the defendant here—defendant Ryan?

A. Yes, I recognize the defendant.

Q. Is that the person who was there?

A. Yes, that is the person.

Q. All right. Then what did you observe happen?

A. Well, there was a noise.

Q. Where was this noise from?

A. Well, I can't tell, in the blind alley like that. You really can't tell.

Q. What did the noise sound like?

A. It could be anything from a firecracker, truck backfiring, or a gunshot. It could be anything—

Q. All right.

A. In that neighborhood, particularly.

Q. Excuse me. When you heard that noise, what was your immediate reaction?

A. He turned around and said, "Somebody is shooting. There is somebody shooting at me." Something like that. And he pulled a pistol from somewhere in front of the car, and he took off.

Q. You are speaking now of Mr. Ryan?

A. Yes.

Q. All right. And when you say he took off, in which direction did he take off?

A. Toward my mother. After he took off, I was wondering what he was running at, and there she was at the end—at the end—toward the right side of the truck.

Q. When you say "the truck," you are referring to your truck?

A. Yeah.

Q. Which was in front of her house, partially?

A. Well, yeah, I guess you could say that.

Q. And when Mr. Ryan took his gun and went toward

your mother's house, is that the first time that you had observed your mother there?

A. She had come down the stairs. I never really observed her until he took off toward her.

Q. All right.

A. Yeah, OK. Yes, that was the first time I had observed her, really.

Q. What did you observe Mr. Ryan do at that time?

A. He had a pistol. He pointed it at her and he said —told her to drop it—cursed and told her to drop it again.

Q. I see. So what did you do?

A. I stopped him from—

Q. Would you describe in what manner you stopped him?

A. Well, he ran past me, and after I saw what was about to happen, I caught up with him, and I grabbed him either around the neck or shoulder—I don't remember —and by the gun hand, and when the gun was against my chest, I looked down and saw that was pointing toward me, you know, about here somewhere [indicating].

Q. You are indicating your throat?

A. Right. So—

Q. Were you holding the hand that had the gun in it?

A. That's right. When I saw this, rather than struggle any further, I just tripped him, just as simple as that.

Q. All right. Could you describe what happened?

A. He fell on his hands and knees.

Q. And what happened to you?

A. Well, he fell on his hands and knees. The weapon —the gun was about three feet from the man that I tripped—Ryan.

Q. Tell us what you did then.

A. I kicked at the weapon, because he was reaching for it.

176

Q. All right. And were you able to kick the weapon itself?

A. I don't know. I was knocked over. I was tackled, literally blocked.

Q. At about the same time?

A. At the same time.

Q. And do you know who it was that tackled or blocked you?

A. Well, the man that I now know as Gillian.

Q. What happened next?

A. I was ordered up against the wall by Gillian.

Q. All right. Now, when you were up against the wall, then what did you observe Mr. Ryan doing?

A. Order—we were admonished, I guess you could say, not to turn around, more or less. But Glen refused to get up against the wall.

Mr. Ehrlich: Repeat that, Mr. Reporter, please.

Answer read by the reporter.

Mr. Ehrlich: Does that mean Glen Bertram?

The witness: That means Glen Bertram.

The district attorney: All right. What did you observe Glen Bertram and Mr. Ryan doing?

A. They were circling each other in the middle of the street, or slightly past the middle of the street on the—other side is where I was.

Q. All right. What, if anything, did Mr. Ryan have in his hand?

A. He had a pistol.

Q. And what, if anything, did Glen Bertram have in his hand?

A. He had a stick.

Q. All right. And then what did you observe happen, could you tell us?

A. Well, they were circling in the street. Also Ryan

177

told the man, "Drop it; Goddamn it, drop it, nigger; I will kill you." Just as simple as that.

Q. All right. What did you observe happen then?

A. He took a swipe at the stick—

Q. Glen?

A. The gun hand—yeah—the gun, yeah, his pistol.

Q. Glen Bertram took a swipe at the gun?

A. Pistol, right.

Q. And he used the stick to do that?

A. Right.

Q. Were you able to tell whether or not he made contact?

A. No, sir, I couldn't say; I wouldn't know.

Q. All right. Then what did you hear happen—or see happen?

A. Well, he circled about ninety degrees, or a quarter of a circle, something like this [demonstrating], and the guy asked him—he asked—Officer Ryan asked him to drop the stick again.

Q. What happened then?

A. Ryan shot and killed Glen Bertram.

Q. At any time during that particular night did you know that Ryan was a police officer?

A. He didn't identify himself at any time as anyone.

Q. Did anyone else present identify him as a police officer to you?

A. No, sir.

Portions of the Cross-Examination

Q. Your name is Ray Dunhill?

A. Yes, that's correct, sir.

Q. Did you ever use any other name?

A. No, sir.

Q. As I understood your testimony this morning, while Mr. Ryan was sitting in his automobile, and while you were standing to the right of his car and about the middle of the right front fender, that he suddenly jumped out of his car and said, "Somebody is shooting at me."

A. He said, "Is someone shooting at me?"

Q. What did he do after he said "Is somebody shooting at me?"

A. Pulled the pistol.

Q. As you say, after he said, "Is somebody shooting at me?" he suddenly had a gun in his hand?

A. Naturally.

Q. And he started toward the end of the alley. Was he running; was he walking?

A. Running. Running.

Q. Running. About how far was he from the end of the alley?

A. About twenty-five feet, I would say.

Q. Did you see your mother standing at the end of the alley?

A. That's correct.

Q. What was she doing?

A. She was standing there. When she recognized what was going on, she stopped.

Q. No, let's take our time now. What was your mother doing?

A. She—well, she was walking from around the front end of the truck, and when she saw the man running toward her with the pistol, she froze.

Q. When did you first see your mother standing there?

A. After he took off and I was seeing who he pointed the gun at.

Q. Had the gun in his hand?

A. He had it in his hand.

Q. He started down the alley?

A. He did.

Q. Toward the end of the alley?

A. Yes.

Q. Had the gun in his hand?

A. He had it pointed.

Q. Aimed or pointed, which?

A. Aimed.

Q. Right at your mother?

A. That's right.

Q. He didn't point at her, he aimed it at her?

A. The gun was aimed.

Q. What was your mother doing?

A. Standing there.

Q. Just standing?

A. Standing there.

Q. Did your mother have her sweater on her left arm or right arm?

A. I think she had her purse and she was just standing there with her hands in front of her. The hands were apparently empty.

Q. You could see her hands?

A. They were apparently empty.

Q. I didn't ask whether they were empty or not. I am asking you whether you could see her hands.

A. I could see them.

Q. She was holding a bag?

A. Right.

Q. Nothing else?

A. That's it.

The court: Just a moment, excuse me.

The witness: No, sir, I wasn't.

The court: Didn't you testify—

The witness: I testified that she had nothing in her hands.

The court: That she had a purse in her hand this morning?

The witness: No, I testified that she had nothing in her hands.

The court: Did you see your mother with the purse?

The witness: That's right, sir.

The court: Where did she have the purse?

The witness: On her arm.

The court: On her arm. Didn't you testify this morning that she had a purse in her hands?

The witness: I testified that I could see her hands were empty.

The court: I thought you said, with the exception of the purse that was in her hands.

The witness: The purse was on her arm.

The court: The purse was on her arm. You didn't say this morning that the purse was on her arm.

The witness: No.

Mr. Ehrlich: Did you see your mother with the gun?

A. I never saw her with a gun.

Q. Well, did you know that your mother owned this gun?

A. No.

Q. Did you at any time say to Mr. Ryan, "That's my mother, she's not shooting at you?"

A. I don't think I said anything to Mr. Ryan. Maybe I did make—I didn't—I don't recall saying anything.

Q. I am asking you. Did you?

A. I don't know.

Q. You don't know?

A. I don't remember.

Q. If your mother had this gun in her hands, you would have seen it, wouldn't you?

A. Definitely.

Q. Do you know that your mother testified several days ago, or last week, that she had loaded this gun a couple of days before the incident; did you know that?

A. No, sir.

Q. There was no conversation about it while you were around there?

181

A. No, sir.

Q. Well, did your mother say anything while you were down there tussling with Mr. Ryan?

A. No, sir.

Q. Well, let's get back. Seeing Ryan running toward your mother, you hopped on his back and grabbed him from the back in some manner?

A. I caught up with him and reached around his neck or shoulder or under his armpit and grabbed him by his pistol hand.

Q. You were holding his hand with a pistol in it?

A. With the pistol in it next to my chest.

Q. Then you tripped him?

A. I tripped him.

Q. Then he fell?

A. He fell.

Q. And he dropped the pistol?

A. He dropped the pistol.

Q. Did you say, referring to your mother, "I think she had a purse in her hand."

A. I don't know, sir.

Q. Will you say you didn't say it?

A. I remember referring to a purse, but I don't know.

Q. Earlier today you were very definite that your mother had a purse in her hand.

A. No, sir, I wasn't.

Q. Now, when Officer Ryan was running toward your mother with his gun in his hand, did he make any remarks? Did he say anything?

A. Yes.

Q. What did he say?

A. "Drop it, Goddamn it, drop it."

Q. "Drop it" what?

A. "Drop it, Goddamn it, drop it."

The court: What did he tell her? "Drop it"—

The witness: Yeah.

The court: "Goddamn it, drop it?"

The witness: Yes.

The court: Thank you.

Mr. Ehrlich: And did your mother drop it?

A. I don't recall. You see a pistol, you don't look for a purse.

The court: I missed that answer.

The witness: I don't know—don't know.

Mr. Ehrlich: Mr. Reporter, please read that answer.

Answer read by the reporter.

The witness: I said if you see—I don't recall—

Q. Did I understand you to say yesterday that you had blood on your head and on your hand—on your finger, I think you said?

A. Yes, sir.

Q. Now, how did you get the blood on your head? Had you fallen when Ryan went down?

A. I was knocked down when he went down.

Q. And when you were knocked down, did that in any way affect your memory as to what happened?

A. I suppose so.

Q. Well now, did it or didn't it?

A. Well, I don't remember.

Q. Mr. Dunhill, do you shave yourself, or does a barber shave you?

A. I shave myself.

Q. Were you closely shaven on the night of the shooting?

A. I shaved that noontime.

Q. When you were wrestling with Mr. Ryan, did you see or feel if he was closely shaven?

A. He had a little beard.

Q. When you say—a little beard, do you mean a slight beard?

A. Yes, sir.

Q. By the way, do you use the same kind of after-shave lotion that you smelled on Mr. Ryan?

A. I use after-shave lotion, but I did not smell any lotion on Mr. Ryan.

Q. You were very close to him?

A. Yes, sir, cheek to cheek for a few moments.

Q. You know that all after-shave lotions have alcohol in them, and that is what gives the tingling feeling when you rub it on?

A. Yes, sir. I didn't smell any alcohol on Mr. Ryan.

Q. I didn't hear your answer.

A. Yes, sir, I didn't smell any alcohol on Mr. Ryan.

It will be observed from a review of the direct and cross-examination of Dunhill that it was necessary to establish that his mother, by going to her home and returning with a pistol and firing it in the direction of Ryan, started a chain of events resulting in the killing of Bertram.

It was also necessary to manage the cross-examination in such manner that Dunhill would be in difficulty about whether he saw his mother shoot in Ryan's direction or what it was she had in her hands, if anything.

By a slow process in the questioning, it became apparent that Dunhill was not telling the truth, and in handling this section of the cross-examination, it was advisable that the judge become involved to the extent where his questions would indicate to the jury that he too believed that Dunhill was lying.

184

Whether Ryan had been drinking the day of the shooting was of great importance. Two witnesses had already testified that he drank nearly a gallon of wine, and one of the witnesses testified particularly that she had quarreled with Ryan, accusing him of smelling of alcohol and that he drank too much wine.

If I had asked Dunhill directly whether there was the odor of alcohol on Ryan's breath or the smell of alcohol around Ryan the answer would have been yes, because all the prosecution witnesses were determined that Ryan be convicted of killing Bertram. But by directing the cross-examination into the innocuous matter of shaving and shaving lotion, Dunhill's answers paralyzed the prosecution and destroyed the base on which the district attorney was building his case.

The secret of good cross-examination is to attack indirectly. The witness is not prepared with rehearsed or organized answers in response to questions. The indirect approach will lull him into a sense of security.

The role of witness represents a frightening experience even for the ordinary honest person. The novelty of the situation, the agitation and hurry which accompany it, the cajolery or intimidation to which a witness is subjected and the confusion of cross-examination—all give rise to important errors and omissions in the testimony.

Part of what a witness sees comes from the object before him. But the larger part of his testimony always comes from his mind. He sees what he wants to see or what he wishes to see.

Dunhill's direct testimony was not challenged question for question. If directly challenged, he would have become angry and would have resented any reflection about the truth of his testimony on direct examination. The more the cross-examiner tries, the more stubborn the witness becomes and the more certain that he is right.

In the Ryan case it was necessary to break down the direct examination and to avoid asking the same questions on cross-examination which were asked on direct. A clear-cut forceful answer by a witness on cross-examination is more deadly in its effect than the same answer given on direct.

It is perhaps needless to add that the jury, after a ten-week trial, found Ryan not guilty. In a discussion of the case with the jurors some days after the verdict, each pointed out that breaking Dunhill was the turning point in the trial. They all agreed that the cross-examination concerning Mrs. Rudd's participation destroyed the prosecution, and when added to the shaving-lotion episode, the drinking by Ryan was dissipated as though it had never happened.

Self-defense by its very nature can be claimed only to justify the killing of one who is the aggressor.

In the Dunhill testimony the evidence showed that Bertram was swinging the stick in an attempt either to hit the gun held by Ryan or to strike Ryan. This conduct was important. It showed that the defendant was actually in fear.

In this case the jury was required to determine which

186

of the two, Bertram or Ryan, was the aggressor at the time of the fatal affray; which one first overstepped the boundaries of the law; which one trespassed on the legal rights of the other; which one by his act and conduct first put himself in the wrong.

Leading Questions

A LEADING or suggestive question is one that suggests to the witness the answer the examiner desires.

On direct examination, leading questions are not allowed, but on cross-examination, leading questions may be propounded as a matter of right. When a witness is hostile, there is little danger in leading questions, for the witness is unlikely to follow the suggested lead.

It is proper to ask leading questions that are designed to lead the witness more quickly to the matter material to the issues. Leading questions may also be properly used in the examination of children unaccustomed to court proceedings, in the removal of ambiguities from expressions used by the witness, and in the examination of witnesses who are slow of comprehension or unfamiliar with English or who are mentally or physically defective.

A judge may, in his discretion, prohibit certain leading questions from being put to an adversary's witness when the witness shows a strong interest or bias in favor of the cross-examining party and needs only an intimation to say whatever is most favorable to that party.

The witness may have purposely concealed such *bias* in favor of one party to induce the other to call him and make him his witness, or the party calling him may be compelled to do so, to prove some single fact necessary to his case.

The leading question must be carefully worded, or the answer may be devastating. In a recent case in Nebraska, the transcript of the trial record has the perfect example of the danger of unprepared leading questions:

Q. Mrs. Jones, on your direct examination you stated that your husband was unkind in his remarks to you.

Now the deadly leading question:

Q. It is a fact, is it not, that he would tell you he loved you?
A. Yes, but it was the way he said it. I would ask him if he loved me, and he would say, "Of course I love you. Can't you get that through your damned fat head?"

A Reasonable Doubt

THE lie can be simple. It can be elaborately structured. It can be honest. It can be malicious.

The lie can fall anywhere—upon any shade of gray or white or black—within its simple definition as a statement contrary to fact.

Exposition of the Lie, the object of defense cross-examination, carries the critical issues of reputation, fortune, and often, life.

A witness' lie can destroy the entire fabric of a prosecution case, which is constructed, much like a building, upon the beams and reinforcing agents of witness testimony.

One emergence of fault, one reasonable doubt, the credibility of the prosecution witness is destroyed, and the veracity of the entire prosecution case is shredded.

Court is much like a football field. The best defense is a good offense. The job of the defense attorney in cross-examination is continually to probe and test for weaknesses in prosecution testimony.

In a criminal case, his latitude in cross-examination is far greater than in civil matters, because the entire focus of our law is on preservation of individual freedom. In the event of an acquittal, there can be no appeal by the prosecution, so the defense has everything to gain by uncompromising cross-examination.

Odds—really—favor the defense, because any witness will lie under repeated cross-examination.

Remember the two basic causes herein before discussed:

1. No two persons will completely agree on what they hear or see in relation to a single incident.

2. No individual will ever remember what he hears or sees in relation to any incident.

Every incident is dominated by sensory perceptions of smell, sight, sound. The relative propensity for the acuteness of these perceptions varies tremendously within individuals at every time and place.

Every incident's reception is tempered by the emotion of its witness, which, in turn, increases the dominant perceptors of smell, sight, and sound and the dominant receptor—memory.

Memory is the built-in fault of testimony. It is never total and varies from testimony to testimony with the same individual.

The juror, aware of his power over a defendant's reputation, fortune, or life, is very sensitive to discovery of the Lie, the one reasonable doubt which he will follow in good conscience.

Caveat

AND now, as a parting word of advice, please bear in mind what Hamlet says in the following expressive lines. Remember that after your professional career is ended, and your final exit made, however eminent you may have been while living, it is possible that some unfeeling grave-digger may bang your skull without *battery* and jestingly proclaim you an *outlaw*:

> ... Why may not that be the skull of a lawyer? Where be his quiddities now, his quillets, his cases, his tenures, and his tricks? Why does he suffer this rude knave now to knock him about the sconce with a dirty shovel, and will not tell him of his action of battery? Hum! This fellow might be in's time a great buyer of land, with his statutes, his recognizances, his fines, his double vouchers, his recoveries: is this the fine of his fines, and the recovery of his recoveries, to have his fine pate full of fine dirt? will his vouchers vouch him no more of his purchases, and double ones too, than the length and breadth of a pair of indentures? The very conveyances of his lands will hardly lie in this box; and must the inheritor himself have no more, ha?